TRE

D0628468

Treasure in Jars of Clay

Nancy George
with Jan Greenough

MONARCH
Crowborough

British Library Cataloguing Data
A catalogue record for this book is available
from the British Library

ISBN 1 85424 387 X

Designed and produced by Bookprint Creative Services
P.O. Box 827, BN21 3YJ, England for
MONARCH PUBLICATIONS
Broadway House, The Broadway
Crowborough, East Sussex TN6 1HQ
Printed in Great Britain

Foreword

I truly believe that Nan and I learned the reality of James 5:16: 'Confess your sins to each other and pray for each other', as far back as 1962. And this transparent openness and agreed praying as found in Matthew 18:19 is what linked our hearts together in tremendous growth and love in our lives. I greatly value our friendship.

As you read Nan's story, I hope you will be able to identify with her through her experiences, and learn the importance of complete trust just as she has done. Our old nature is very stubborn and independent, and trusting someone else is one of the hardest things to do in our Christian life. But no matter how hard we try to do things our own way, we will fail until we learn the sufficiency of Christ through total dependence on him. May you learn, as she did, to submit and obey, so that your life may be one of peace and fulfilment.

Drena Verwer
Operation Mobilisation

Prologue

In the hot summer of 1963 my life was as full as I'd ever hoped it would be: I was twenty-four, independent, working in Europe—and in love!

Two years previously I had left my home in the United States and sailed for Spain to join a Christian student movement called Operation Mobilisation. Operation Mobilisation has since become an established missionary force, with currently 1,900 adults working in 40 countries and on board the ships *Doulos* and *Logos II*. Several thousand more young people join OM during the summer for the Love Europe programme. It was the start of a great adventure in faith which has shaped my life ever since. I left home with the blessing of my family, who were delighted that I was going into full-time Christian work, and with the prayers of many members of my home church, who pledged to support me financially with regular gifts of money.

I worked initially in a team of five, travelling around Spain and visiting Protestant churches, challenging young people to give us a few weeks of their summer holidays. We planned to take them to Italy, where they would find the culture similar to their own, but where they would have more freedom to speak about their Christian faith openly. This experience, we felt, would help them to live out their faith at home.

We also visited houses, offering Christian literature and inviting people to enrol in a Bible correspondence course. There was a huge response.

Over the months the work expanded as young people from all over Europe gathered to go out in small teams. We had prayed for a hundred workers to help us: soon we had two hundred. The fruits of their activities threatened to swamp us: 8,000 replies from Italy, 5,000 from France, 4,000 from Austria and Germany and many more from England, Holland and Belgium. The need for office staff became urgent, and as I'd had some secretarial experience, I volunteered to work as secretary to the director, George Verwer, and his wife Drena. George was an old friend from the States, and Drena and I became very close.

We set up headquarters in the Netherlands, from where we distributed literature: gospels, leaflets, and manuals for team leaders. We also co-ordinated the training programmes and the placements for the teams.

Among the staff who joined us was a young civil engineer called Ron George. Ron had interrupted his studies to travel around the Mediterranean with OM, leading a team to North Africa to investigate the opportunities for evangelism among Muslims. I typed George's letter to Ron, asking him to return to Europe and help us that summer: we needed to prepare for 1,000 young people working in five countries and many languages.

It was my job to collect Ron from the station. Emerging from the stream of travellers was a tall, handsome young man with a diffident smile. I liked him at once, and was sure we were going to get along, though I had no thoughts of romance—life was far too busy.

However, as I got to know him better, I found myself thinking about him more and more. I liked his quiet, clear English voice, and the way he always went straight to the heart of things. His scientific training made him impatient with waffle, and his words were always direct and to the point. There was no evasiveness or sham in him: I knew he was someone I could trust totally.

I enjoyed his company, and it was tempting to arrange to share duties with such an attractive companion, though we always worked in groups. We seemed to be on the same wavelength. Ron and I shared the same sense of humour, and often in meetings I would see his warm brown eyes full of laughter, turning to me as one who would surely share the joke.

I respected his deep commitment to the Lord Jesus, and his willingness to turn his hand to any task that would help in the work of spreading the good news of the gospel. His was a mature faith, beside which my own periods of rebellion and confusion seemed childish. Back in the States I'd dropped out of the Moody Bible Institute, which I found to be too safe and enclosed a Christian world, rather like my home. Instead I chose to work and earn enough money to put myself through an ordinary secular college, where I studied psychology and English. I had come to hate the sugar-coated Christianity I was offered at home. I didn't exactly hate God, but I gave him a bad time! It was after this that I took the post with OM. I enjoyed the work, and my faith blossomed in the more robust atmosphere of mission. George and Drena watched over me lovingly as I made my way back to full commitment to Jesus Christ.

9

It was to Jesus that I now took the problem of my feelings about Ron.

'What do you want me to do, Lord? Is this really the man I'm to spend the rest of my life with? Everything about him seems so perfect: I respect him, I'm attracted to him, I'm in love with him—yet he's never given any sign that he thinks of me as any more special than the other girls.'

That, of course, was another problem. Neither had I given him any sign of my feelings—it would hardly be suitable. We were both team leaders, charged with the pastoral care of groups of young people who looked to us for guidance. And Ron's dark good looks and shy manner made him popular with everyone. The same week that I first prayed about my relationship with Ron, two girls on my team came to me separately for counselling. They each said more or less the same thing.

'What am I to do, Nan? I think I'm in love with the leader of the boys' team, Ron George. Should I tell him? How can I know if it's God's will that we should be together?'

It was tempting to say, 'Search me! I've got the same problem!' But of course I couldn't. I told them both to be patient and see whether their feelings changed—and that it was the worst kind of blackmail to say to anyone, 'I think it's God's will that we love each other.' But I found it harder than ever to contain my own feelings. I found myself watching Ron when he was with the girls, trying to detect any difference in his manner.

Meanwhile we all worked frantically—sometimes in shifts through the night—churning out manuals in five languages for the July conference. My main task was to organise registration for all the participants.

After the conference I was to take a team of fifteen girls to Spain for three months, travelling in a jeep and two cars. As the time drew near, I began to look forward to getting away from administration and back out on the road with a team, though I was rather apprehensive about being responsible for three vehicles. My idea of the internal combustion engine was something you kicked if it didn't start.

The conference seemed to fly by, but as usual I was so busy that I hadn't had time to make my own preparations for the team. On the final day I was rushing about, trying to organise the loading of literature and camping equipment, when I met Ron in the literature depot.

'Penny for your thoughts, Nan,' he said.

I looked up at him in surprise.

'Sorry, I didn't realise I was so preoccupied,' I said. 'To be honest, I'm worried about this trip. I don't know anything about cars, and I've never put up a tent in my life. How on earth am I going to manage?'

'I used to be a scout master and I loved it,' he replied. 'Come on, let's go back to the tents and dismantle them together. Then I'll show you how to pitch one.'

He made it look encouragingly easy and after my lesson it took me just fifteen minutes to pitch the tent.

'Right, now for the cars,' he said brightly. Where are your other drivers? We'll go and have a lesson in mechanics!'

The cars were parked in an open field, surrounded by boxes of literature and baggage. I watched as Ron pointed out the basics to Karen and Sue, the other drivers, then turned to the jeep.

The others continued loading as he opened the bonnet and checked the oil and water.

'It's really quite simple,' he said. 'You need to know how to take out the spark plugs at least.'

As we bent, heads together, over the engine, I reached to take out a spark plug, but his large hand covered mine and moved it away from the grease. Then, without warning, he whispered, 'Nan, will you pray about being my wife?'

He said nothing more, offered no explanation. I pulled my hand away and wondered if I had heard right.

He cleared his throat nervously. 'I know it's going to be a busy summer for you. But please, will you pray about marrying me?'

I looked up at him in astonishment. Until that moment we had never been alone together, never so much as held hands. Yet how like Ron to go right to the heart of the matter without any preliminaries! Stirred by his honesty I looked down at his strong hand, urgently clasping mine over the dirty engine.

'I've already been praying about it for nearly a year,' I answered. 'Yes, I will!'

A huge grin of relief broke over his face, and we stood for a moment trying to let the realisation sink in. We loved each other.

Then I broke the silence.

'We'd better go and tell Drena and George— they'll never believe it!'

We ran hand in hand across the field to the main building, and raced upstairs two at a time to the Verwers' room. Ron knocked quietly at the door and we smiled at the surprise we were about to deliver.

Drena opened the door and took one look at us. Then she threw one arm around Ron, the other round me, and exclaimed, 'I knew it! I just knew it! When are you two getting married?'

Chapter 1

It was a mild and sunny September day, one year later, and our old blue Volkswagen van was jolting its way over the mountains of Yugoslavia. Stretched out comfortably on a mattress in the back, I could hear the protesting squeak of the springs, the uneven roar of the engine, and Ron whistling cheerfully as he drove. We were going home!

That year had been one of change and adaptation for both of us. Throughout our nine-month engagement and the first three months of our marriage, the most difficult task had been to find time for each other. After announcing our engagement we had gone to Spain, separately, and the rest of our courtship was conducted by letter. In fact, Ron was convinced that this was a bonus: he was shy and diffident, and found it hard to express himself. Face to face he easily became tongue-tied, but when he wrote he had time to think about what he wanted to say. I treasured each letter he sent.

On our return it was decided that we should both take teams to work in Iran for a year. We were delighted to be going to the same country, but in a Muslim society we didn't have the chance to spend much time together—Ron travelled through the towns and villages distributing Bibles, while I taught English in Tehran.

We were married in June in Tehran, surrounded by friends from OM. I wore a borrowed wedding gown, and Ron looked shyer than ever in his one good suit. We each sent home a set of photographs—my parents in the US had never met Ron, and his family in England had not met me.

We'd both found our time in Iran exciting, but hard work—partly because of the inevitable pre-wedding nerves, and partly because of the nature of Islamic culture. I found the role of women in that society restricting and frustrating, and I was happy to be returning to the West where my energy could have free rein! One of the greatest joys of our marriage was our shared commitment to mission. Working for God had brought us together, and it was wonderful to know that our future was in his hands. There had been talk of us going to India with the Verwers. Excited as we were by the prospect, we felt that it was an extra blessing to go as man and wife, to share all the work, the joys and sorrows and love in store for us.

In all the bustle of finishing up our work and saying goodbye to friends in Iran, life had been fairly hectic. Now we were going home, looking forward to our holiday, and the journey looked like our first real chance to spend time alone together.

However, our party had grown as we travelled. Just before leaving Tehran we met two young Pakistani men who needed a lift from Iran to Germany where they were going to work. Then, when we reached Istanbul, where we spent the night with friends, we were joined by two English girls, also on their way back to Europe after spending a year with OM. So it was a party of four who joined us on the romantic night stop we made among the vineyards of Bulgaria, and shared our breakfast of great black grapes given to us by a local farmer. It wasn't quite the honeymoon we had planned!

Ron and I shared the driving, so I sat beside him in the front of the van, while the others sat or lay on the mattresses we had spread out in the back, over the engine. We couldn't be alone, but at least I wanted that place beside him, as his wife. Nevertheless, after a while I felt that perhaps I was being rather selfish in guarding my position so jealously—it did happen to be the most comfortable seat! So when we stopped around noon that day, I offered to move into the back, and the two girls took my place.

I stretched luxuriously and yawned, warmed by the sun filtering through the grimy windows. For a while I watched the countryside unfolding—great cornfields giving way to hills, and hills to the rocky terrain of the mountains. I dozed for a while. When I awoke, we were descending again towards the plains, and Ron was wrestling with the steering as the road wound precipitously past outcrops of brown rock. I reached into my handbag for my Bible. It was several days since I'd had the chance of a proper quiet time of prayer and study, and I was reading the Resurrection story: the suffering, death and life of Jesus Christ. The final words of Jesus were important to me: 'The Christ will suffer and rise from the dead on the third day, and repentance and forgiveness of sins will be preached in his name to all nations' (Lk 24:46, 47). Bound up in that Great Commission, I reflected, was God's plan for our life, and the future towards which we were driving so hopefully.

In 1964 the roads near the Yugoslavian border were

not made up—they were rough dirt tracks—and we made our way over the mountains with the van lurching and bumping along the uneven winding lanes. As we swerved round one particularly sharp bend, I saw the top fly off the water carrier which was strapped to the back of the driver's seat. It was surrounded by everyone's luggage and by all our wedding gifts (everything we jointly owned was travelling with us in the van) so I hurriedly got up to replace it. I didn't want everything spoiled by the water that was beginning to splash out.

That was the last thing I really remember clearly. The front wheels of the van dropped down into a deep rut in the road, causing the vehicle to shudder as I bent, unsupported, over the luggage.

It was the whiplash of that sudden jolt that broke my neck.

The rut was uneven and the van tipped sideways. I was thrown out of the side door into the ditch that ran between the road and the mountainside, and my face hit the dirt with a thud. The van finished up leaning against the side of the hill, with the bumper pinning my thigh to the ground.

I have no idea how long it took the others to extricate themselves from the van. I lay there with my face in the earth and I could feel nothing: my body had ceased to exist. I knew I must be dying.

'Lord, take me home,' I prayed. 'I'm finally right there at heaven's gate—I'm ready, I want to go all the way. Just take me on home.'

It wasn't a sad prayer—simply a logical one. The promise of heaven was very precious to me, and I was sure I was about to die. I was content, in that moment, to rest in the arms of the Father.

Then I felt myself being pulled along the ground.

Somehow the three men had managed to lift the back of the van and pull me clear. I was unable to move, but into my restricted view of sky and hillside there suddenly appeared Ron's face, and at once my prayer changed. I knew, then, that I couldn't die.

'Oh, no, Lord, that's not fair,' I thought. 'Please keep me alive for Ron's sake. It's not fair to him; we've only been married for three months and he loves me. Just keep me alive—not for my sake but for Ron's.'

I still believe that is just what happened: I was kept alive for my husband's sake.

I knew that I must be badly injured, but I was in no pain. My feet and legs felt as though they were miles away from me, but I never thought that my neck might be broken. All I was concerned about right then was whether I was decent! I was wearing my favourite dress—a fashionably short black and white one, with a black belt, and although I had no sensation in my limbs I was aware of just how short that dress was.

'Am I decent?' I kept saying to Ron. 'Are my legs decent?'

He straightened my legs and tidied my dress, but he was desperately worried. We had travelled all morning without seeing another car, and he couldn't imagine how we were going to get help.

However, within a few minutes several cars had stopped, and a small crowd gathered. A woman came up and spoke to Ron in French, and he explained what had happened in his version of her language— part broken French, part bluff. I remember wishing he wouldn't spend so much time practising his French but come back and tell me what was going on. At last she drove off and Ron came back to my side.

'She's a pharmacist, Nan, not a doctor, but she says no one is to move you. She's gone to get help.'

I was immensely relieved. I knew that we were in the middle of nowhere, and that for miles we had passed no people, no towns, no other traffic. Yet five minutes later a Yugoslavian ambulance arrived: it had been following us through the mountains.

Everything then seemed to happen very fast. Two men climbed out and loaded me onto a stretcher. Ron left our friends in charge of the van and our luggage, and got into the ambulance with me. One of the ambulance men explained that we were going to the nearest town, Nis, where there was a hospital.

Ron sat beside me in the ambulance. I saw him put out his hand and lean towards me, as though he were grasping my hand in his, but I could feel nothing.

'Ron, hold my hand,' I said.

'I'm holding it, Nan,' he replied. I could see the concern in his eyes.

'I can't feel you. Please hold me.' Strangely, I wasn't frightened or panicky. It was as if the numbness of my body extended to my mind also. I could speak and think clearly, yet I didn't question why I was unable to feel. It was as though part of my brain refused to consider what was happening. I simply existed—lying on a stretcher in an ambulance, jolting along a road. I don't know whether it was the effect of shock, or some way the mind has of protecting itself by ignoring things, but I didn't think ahead. I was thankful to have Ron beside me. He lifted his hand and gently brushed some dirt from my cheek, and wiped away some blood from a cut on my lip.

'Ron! I can feel that! I can feel your hand!' He smiled, and went on stroking my face, and moving strands of my long hair off my forehead. It was soothing and reassuring to feel his touch.

Nis was a small market town, and its hospital was a

dull, unimposing building. I caught a glimpse of its grey walls as the ambulance turned a corner and stopped. Then my stretcher was placed on a trolley and I was wheeled in through the swing doors.

The hospital seemed very crowded and busy. From my restricted position I could hear hurrying feet and loud, unintelligible voices, and doctors in white coats passed on the periphery of my vision. The smell was the same as hospitals everywhere—heavily antiseptic, enlivened in places by a gust of fresh air from an open window, or by the stale smell of cooked food as we passed a room where patients were eating a meal. I felt slightly dizzy watching the lights on the corridor ceiling pass overhead, so I kept my eyes on Ron as he walked beside me. I was glad he was there—not least because of his ability to communicate with people. Ron can bluff his way in any language, whether known to him or not, and I knew I couldn't even ask for a drink in Serbo-Croat, let alone discuss my condition with a doctor.

We were left in a cubicle, and a nurse came in, removed my clothes and covered me with a sheet.

'Ron, I'm terribly thirsty. Do you think she can get me a drink of water?'

Ron mimed and asked for water in two or three unlikely-sounding languages, and sure enough, the nurse disappeared and came back with water. She was followed by two doctors who examined me at some length, feeling my limbs for broken bones and occasionally looking at my face for some reaction. I could feel nothing, so I gave them an encouraging smile. Then they stood beside the trolley murmuring in low voices—quite unnecessarily, as we were unable to understand a word.

After some debate, the nurse was sent off, clearly to

fetch something. She returned carrying a large metal frame, padded in places. With some difficulty they fixed this over my head and shoulders, so that it clamped over my chest and held my head still. The doctors didn't seem to know what to do for me, though they obviously realised that my neck was fractured somehow. The brace, we realised afterwards, was not the right solution; it did nothing to help my condition, and after a day or so it caused pressure sores on my chin and the back of my head. But the language problem made it difficult to ask the medical staff what they were planning, or their reasons for doing things. All we could do was trust them.

Now for the first time I began to feel really uncomfortable. The brace held rigid the only part of my body that I could move, so that my head and neck were stiff. It was heavy and hard and made me feel as though I were behind bars. At last a tiny part of my mind began to awake, and I became aware that I was helpless—really helpless and unable to control anything. Yet still I didn't think about the implications: I didn't wonder how long I would be like this, or what was wrong with me. Unafraid, I lived in each moment as it came, like a child or a sick animal, unquestioning.

After some time I was moved into a small room containing four beds. The one next to mine was occupied by an old woman who was breathing heavily. Ron sat down in the chair beside my bed and looked at me.

'Nan, I'm starving. Will you be all right for a bit while I go and find some food? I think I saw a kiosk down by the gate as we came in.'

'Sure I will—but don't be too long.'

He came back with bread and chocolate which he ate hungrily.

'Want some?'

'No, thanks, but I'm awfully thirsty again.'

'I'll go and find some more water for you.'

And off he went again, returning triumphantly with a pitcher of water.

Ron slept that night in the chair by my bed, waking whenever I seemed restless, and patiently feeding me sips of water, or moistening my dry lips. I dozed off and on. I was in no pain, but my body felt heavy and uncomfortable, and sometimes I was breathless. Still I felt no concern for my situation, no panic. I considered the dimly-lit room with a kind of detached interest. The brace held me so that I could no longer turn my head, but I was aware of a window on one side of me, beyond Ron's chair, and of a door on the other side, beyond the old woman's bed. Towards dawn I must have slept more deeply, for when I woke fully the room was light, and the bed beside me was empty.

'Where's the old lady, Ron? Where did she go?' I asked drowsily.

'She fell asleep,' Ron replied. I was too weary and confused to notice his evasiveness. When he wasn't standing directly in front of me I couldn't see his face, so I couldn't tell how deeply disturbed he was. The woman had died in the night, and somehow I had slept through the ensuing commotion. Ron, emerging now from his own shock after the accident, realised for the first time the situation we were in, and that I might die, too. He is by nature a direct person, and usually his words are blunt and to the point, but he knew he didn't want me to face the thought of death right then. So for the next few days, until I finally began to come to a full awareness of what had happened, he struggled to hide his feelings from me, and bore alone the knowledge that the balance between my life and death was very precarious.

Lying in the hospital bed that morning, I wondered whether we should contact my parents and tell them about the accident. Perhaps there was no need to worry them, I thought: perhaps I would be up and about again before long.

I was born in 1939 in Colorado, USA, the youngest of nine children: three of the older ones had by then enlisted in the armed forces, and I knew them mostly from photographs and their brief visits home. The rest of us were a tightly knit family. The first six children were born during the Depression, and Dad worked long hours on his father's farm to support us all. Mum never seemed to stop washing, ironing, cooking, batch-baking and bottling. She had the ability to make work seem like play, and each of us had our daily tasks as soon as we were out of babyhood. She loved action, moved like a whirlwind, and any chore we skimped she would re-do perfectly, at once. We learned early to obey and co-operate: to complain was a fruitless exercise.

My parents had always been strict disciplinarians, who lived by their own rigid moral code. I gathered from my older brothers and sisters that Dad had a fiery temper, but I seldom saw any sign of it; by the time I came on the scene not only was he an older man, but both my parents had become Christians. They added the rules of the local Baptist church to their already firm regime: the cinema, dancing and pop music were all forbidden to us. My brother Larry was only thirteen months older than me, and we were often taken for twins. In childhood we competed in everything, rope-skipping, friendships, measles and mumps. In adolescence, however, Larry rebelled, and actually went to the High School dances. I was shocked, but I kept his secrets.

Our childhood was happy, secure, and busy. In summer we picked dandelions by the hundreds for Grandma's wine. Before going swimming we weeded (and picked) the strawberries, hoping the tell-tale red stains would wash away in the pool. During the bottling season we recruited as many friends as possible to help string runner beans, shred cabbage for sauerkraut, shuck corn and (what I hated most) pod peas. Mum gave prizes for competitions, we sang songs and told riddles to help the work along. It was neighbourhood practice each summer for any bored or idle friends to make their way to the Sheppards' back porch and garden to join in the fun. The reward for all our hard work was to go and admire the gleaming rows of jars on the cellar shelves, and the pride with which we fetched them one by one throughout the winter months for eating.

I remembered the fun we had in our big family: Ruth, the eldest, was separated from me by eighteen years, and by Bill, Betty, Lyle, Marian, Keith, Pat and Larry. We were all encouraged to take music lessons; Larry disliked the piano and was allowed to give it up, but Pat and I continued for years. I tried my hand at drums for a while, but eventually the family persuaded me that this was not a ladylike pursuit. As the baby of the family, I seemed always to be running to keep up with the others, trying to be as pretty as Pat, as active as Larry.

As I lay still in my bed, I remembered Pat pushing me on our tyre swing in the yard. I could almost feel the cool breeze fanning my face, as Pat pushed harder, then suddenly I was sailing through the air, pigtails flying, to land, swing and all, in an untidy heap in the dust. Larry had climbed the tree and untied the swing rope from the branch, hoping that the momentum would be sufficient for me to land in the stream at the edge of the garden. I was dazed and frightened, but I didn't dare cry hard or Pat and Larry would be reprimanded. Even Larry's mischief couldn't shake my strong sense of family loyalty.

Thinking of my active, busy childhood, I sighed. It was irksome to be immobilised like this; I hoped the doctors would come soon and sort out my problems.

Later that morning two doctors did arrive, one of whom spoke some English. They took pins and began to prick my feet and legs.

'You feel this?' they asked at intervals, presumably each time they moved the pins.

'No, nothing.'

'And here?'

'No.'

I could tell where the pin was pressing into me only by where the doctors stood. I concentrated my mind towards what seemed the right part of my body, but I was aware of nothing. Half way up—was he pricking my elbow or my waist? I couldn't tell.

'You feel this?'

'No.'

At last they reached my shoulders.

'Yes!—But I could have told you that,' I added, 'I've been feeling this beastly hard brace there all night.'

'Very well. We will come back and see you later.' And they left.

'Nan?' It was Ron's voice.

'I can't see you there, Ron. Lean over so I can see you.'

'Is that better? Are you all right?'

He was worried, of course, because now it had all been spelled out for me. The tests showed that I had no feeling at all below my shoulders, and I was quite unable to move. I think he expected to see realisation on my face, but the merciful smothering unawareness was still there. Ron could tell from the first glance that I still had no idea how seriously I was injured. He had spent the latter part of the night in agonised prayer, trying to come to terms with the possibility that I might die, and the probability that I would be totally paralysed. My reply was typical.

'Sure, honey, I'm fine—under the circumstances. Any chance of another sip of water?'

After a while Ron made another foray to the kiosk at the gate for food for himself. A nurse came in and offered me lunch but I still couldn't face eating. When Ron returned, he looked excited.

'I've been talking to the doctors, Nan. They want to transfer you to Belgrade.'

'Belgrade? That's right up in the north, isn't it? Why?'

'There's an orthopaedic clinic where you can get proper treatment. It'll be much better than here— well, from what I've seen, almost anything would be better than here.'

It was true—the hospital was rather spartan, the equipment seemed to us to be old-fashioned, and even allowing for the difficulties of the language barrier, it was hard to find out what was going on. On the whole we were rather relieved at the prospect of transfer to a larger, more modern hospital.

Ron had to go back in a police car to the scene of the accident, to collect the rest of our party, whom he had left guarding our belongings, and to drive the van back to Nis. All four of the others were unhurt, and they continued their journey by train. First, however, the girls managed to contact another OM worker, who informed our head office of our situation.

Ron spent another night on the chair by my bed, and on the second morning after the accident I was again loaded onto a stretcher, still wearing the metal brace.

'There are two nurses going with you, Nan,' Ron told me. 'I'm going to follow you in the van, so I'll see you in Belgrade.'

'Drive carefully, then,' I replied. 'And before you go, will you tell the doctor how much I hate cigarette smoke? Can you get him to ask the nurses not to smoke in the ambulance?'

Ron spoke to the doctor, who certainly said something to the two male nurses who lifted me into the vehicle, but nevertheless they lit up as soon as the doors were closed, and they puffed away throughout the journey. I didn't realise then how dangerous cigarette smoke could be for someone with possible paralysis of the lungs; at the time I merely found it very unpleasant.

That trip was a nightmare. The ambulance travelled very fast, so that Ron, following in the van, found it impossible to keep up. He tried hard to keep within sight of the ambulance, averaging 120 kilometres an hour, but often he lost us. Every time we came into a village or a town the driver switched on the siren, which would keep sounding until we came out into the countryside again. The ear-splitting wail of that siren seemed to go on endlessly.

When the driver decided it was time for a coffee break, he pulled over to the side of the road and all three men got out.

'Please,' I said in English, 'leave the doors open.' Somehow I made them understand, and leaving the rear doors wide open, they went off together. I wanted to be able to call out if I needed help (though I had no idea if they stayed within earshot), and I desperately wanted some fresh air. They were gone for perhaps fifteen minutes, but it seemed like an age. The smoky atmosphere inside thinned a little, and a warm breeze ruffled my hair. Never was I so grateful to breathe clean air. It was very quiet; occasionally a car or a lorry would pass by with a rush, rocking the ambulance slightly. Through the open doors I could hear birds singing. For a while I felt very abandoned and alone, lying helpless in the empty vehicle, but I was also relieved to have a break from the incessant incomprehensible chatter of the nurses and their smoking. In spite of my impossible situation, the uselessness of my inert body, the discomfort of the brace and my growing anxiety about what lay ahead, I relaxed and enjoyed the respite.

Then it was over; the nurses, still waving cigarettes, climbed back in and slammed the doors. The driver started the engine with a roar and we drove on again, bumping and lurching on the rough roads with the siren shrieking.

After what seemed like hours, one of the men broke off his conversation and said something to me, gesticulating at the window. I could see nothing but the ceiling and the faces of the nurses, but the ambulance was slowing down and I guessed what he meant: we had arrived at the orthopaedic clinic in Belgrade.

Chapter 2

Once again my trolley-bed was lowered from the ambulance; once again I was pushed through the wide doors into a hospital and along seemingly endless corridors; once again I passed porters and nurses who talked incomprehensibly about me. I had a growing feeling of nightmare—all this had happened already, in Nis, and now it was all happening again, in Belgrade. The slow dawning of awareness which had begun on the journey suddenly clarified. I was helpless and alone in a foreign country, unable to speak or understand the language. Just as my body was paralysed, in a sense—for I love to talk—so was my voice: I couldn't communicate any more than I could move. The sense of isolation overwhelmed me.

The two days since the accident seemed like a bad dream: I'd been cocooned by a sense of unreality, unquestioning and accepting whatever happened. I felt different now, as my trolley clattered through a door and into a huge, brightly lit room. I was alone; Ron was somewhere behind me on the road to Belgrade, unable to help, or speak for me, or take care of me. I had been cushioned by the deep sense of security Ron's presence always gave me: now he was

29

gone, I felt utterly alone and afraid. For the first time my reserve broke: tears gathered in my eyes and began to trickle uncomfortably sideways down my face.

A doctor bent over me. Alerted by the hospital in Nis, he had stayed on beyond his duty hours to await my arrival. Through my tears I saw a smiling square face with fair hair.

'Hello, Nan-cee,' he said, with an unfamiliar inflection in my name. 'I am Dr Simic.'

I was amazed and relieved. 'You speak English!' I cried.

'Certainly. I studied at Stoke Mandeville Hospital in England, so I speak English quite well. And we are going to find out how to help you, yes?'

'Doctor, is my husband here yet?'

He murmured a question to a nurse, and replied,

'Not yet, but you will see him when he arrives. Now, first we are going to take some X-rays, so we can find out what is the damage.'

He helped one of the nurses to unfasten the brace, and gradually his disapproving mutterings turned to real anger.

'Look at this—and this! It is all unnecessary—quite wrong.'

The brace had grazed my forehead and the back of my head, and the bar under my chin had rubbed and chafed my skin during the jolting ambulance ride until it had cut deeply into the flesh. When he saw the sores he began talking very fast and furiously in his own language to the nurses, and slammed the brace down angrily onto a table. However, when he turned back to me his voice softened again.

'We must lift you onto the X-ray table, Nancy—are you ready?'

'Sure—any time.' I couldn't understand his gentleness—I had no feeling in most of my body, so it didn't seem to matter much what they did to me. I was totally unprepared for the sickening jolt of pain which shot through my neck when I was lifted. For two days I had been held rigid by the brace, and now the slightest movement was agonising. I screamed—and kept on screaming.

It wasn't just the spasm in my neck muscles causing the pain; Dr Simic could see that I was suffering more than a simple fracture of the vertebra. Blood had begun collecting between my skull and my skin, so that my face was grotesquely swollen. My eyes were black and the discolouration had spread almost down to the jaw on both sides. Whatever was causing it, the pressure and bruising had developed to a degree that any movement sent a bolt of pain through my whole head.

Suddenly the door burst open and there stood Ron, red-faced and panting. He had arrived at the main door of the hospital, heard my screams, and come racing through the corridors, following the sound, to find me! Immediately my panic and fear subsided, and I managed a shaky smile. He grabbed my hand— then, remembering that I couldn't feel it, put his hands on my shoulders.

'It's OK, Nan, I'm here. It's all right. What's going on?'

Dr Simic began patiently explaining all over again about the X-rays, which had to be taken before he could go off duty.

'Ron—before they start—can they get me a drink?'

'Of course, Nancy,' interposed Dr Simic. 'What would you like?'

'Well—best of all, I guess I'd like a Coca-Cola.'

'I'm afraid we don't have Coca-Cola here in Yugoslavia—is there anything else?'

I really did want something with a strong flavour—somehow plain water never seemed to slake the parching thirst I'd had since the accident—and the only thing I could think of was Grape-ep, a fizzy drink we had in the States.

'I know that one—I think we can find something similar for you,' and he spoke rapidly to a nurse.

Nothing ever tasted so good as that sweet sparkling drink after the long smoky journey and all my crying.

There followed a long and uncomfortable session as I was X-rayed from every possible angle. Ron was helping the nurses to lift me when suddenly Dr Simic exploded again into a torrent of angry Serbo-Croat. My eyes flew to Ron's face for an explanation, but he looked as bemused as I was. After a while the doctor calmed down enough to revert to English for our benefit.

'The accident happened on Wednesday, yes?'

'That's right—about lunch-time,' Ron volunteered.

'And how often has she been turned since?'

'Turned? You mean on to her side or front? Not at all. She's been lying on her back ever since.'

'Look—look at this! It is a disgrace! It need never have happened.'

Ron looked and saw a huge bedsore on my bottom, about two inches across. It seemed that the hospital staff at Nis, unsure of the extent of the damage, had simply taken care not to move me and risk making my condition worse. Unfortunately, for a paralysed person, two days without changing position causes dreadful damage to the skin at any pressure points. There

32

was a similar sore on the back of my head where the brace had rubbed.

'She will go onto a ripple bed,' snapped Dr Simic. 'We will try to repair this—this unnecessary damage.'

There was more agonising lifting as I was taken from the X-ray room and moved to an empty double room further along the corridor, and placed on a ripple bed. This blissful machine was rather like a water bed, but it was gently vibrated by an electric motor so that the rippling motion would ensure that no further pressure sores developed. I realised that for the first time in two days I felt comfortable, and the gentle movement of the bed was very soothing.

Dr Simic followed us to our room, and explained that Ron could use the second bed.

'I have to go off duty now, for the weekend. On Monday I will see the X-rays and decide what to do. I will speak with you then.'

And he left, closing the door behind him.

'I guess they'll wait for the weekend to see if I live or die,' I remarked wryly to Ron. But I had no intention of dying right then—all I wanted was to be lulled gently off to sleep by that wonderful bed.

It was not until much later that Ron told me about that night. While I slept, he was given a meal by one of the nurses, and then he fetched his small suitcase from the van. He sat down on his bed to open it. Lying on top of his clothes was the album containing our wedding photos, and slowly he turned the pages. There we were, only three months before, so happy and full of hope, sure that God had planned a bright and active future for us together. Ron looked at the girl in the picture, radiant in a white dress, with her long hair piled up elegantly, smiling at the camera. Then he turned to look at me, lying helpless in the bed beside him, unable to move, my face swollen and black with congested blood, my long hair matted with blood and dirt. Very quietly, so as not to wake me, he began to cry—in a halting, awkward way at first, and then more easily, as the tension drained out of him with his tears. The bed rocked with his sobs, as he whispered,

'Why, God? Why have you let this happen to us? Where is your plan for us now? I know you haven't forsaken us—but give us the strength to hold on to your promises through all this.'

He sat for a long while beside me, as the evening passed and night came. The hospital grew quiet; only a dim light burned in the corridor outside our room. Ron sat on in the darkness clutching the album of photographs that was the symbol of the old life we had left behind. He searched for prayers to express his sense of loss, trying to reaffirm his faith in a loving Father.

All light had faded from the window, but no stars could be seen in the night sky tinged with the glare from the city. 'Though I walk in the valley of the shadow of death, I will fear no evil; thy rod and thy staff will comfort me...' What if Nan dies? What if she can never walk again? Ron thought. Still, everything—even this accident—is under God's control. We won't be afraid. As long as we're following Christ, the shepherd will lead us to green pastures. Then he recalled the words of an old chorus, 'He gives more grace as the burdens grow greater, He adds more strength as the burdens increase.' Could it be true? Would we be given strength? We had to keep in touch with Jesus, for he was waiting to fill us with his grace.

I never really knew what Ron suffered in his vigil of weeping and prayer that night, but I never saw him despairing. The next day he looked haggard and white, but there was a determined light in his eyes, as though he had faced the worst, alone, and come out of it trusting even more firmly in God's love for us.

We spent the whole weekend in that darkened room, much as we had in Nis—I dozed intermittently and rested, and Ron fetched me drinks of water, read, talked, and slept. We didn't discuss the future. We waited.

On Monday morning Dr Simic arrived early, looked in on us, found me still alive, and went to see the X-rays. After a while he came back and we looked at him expectantly.

'I have looked—I have seen what needs to be done. The operation I could do here—it is my special area, this spinal injury. But afterwards, you will need special care, rehabilitation. It would be better for you to go to England for the whole thing. Stoke Mandeville Hospital has better equipment than we have here, better facilities—everything.' He looked at Ron. 'This operation—it can wait maybe twenty-four hours, no longer. Nancy must be moved to England at once. I suggest that you go to your embassies—the US and the British embassies are both here in Belgrade—they will help you get her on a flight to England immediately.'

Ron grabbed his coat.

'I'll go right away. Don't worry, Nan—we'll soon have you safe home.'

I smiled at him, but my heart sank. I couldn't bear the thought of being moved again. I felt I could endure anything here, even if the facilities were not so good, as long as I didn't have to travel. Besides, I had a growing trust in Dr Simic. Though he was head of

35

the whole department, his bedside manner was superb. He never seemed in a hurry, and was always willing to give his time to his patients. As the door closed behind Ron, he sat down on the empty bed.

'And now—we talk. What is worrying you?'

It was a strange thing—until then I had been careful to ask no questions. I hadn't asked anyone exactly what was wrong, nor whether the paralysis would go away, nor what my future might be. I had avoided asking such questions even in my own mind. But just as I had first begun to feel fear and apprehend my real situation as I entered the Belgrade clinic alone, so now that Ron had left, I began to face reality squarely. It was as though while Ron was taking care of me—nursing me and interpreting for me—I was also taking care of him, trying to protect him and myself from thinking the unthinkable.

Now, lying there alone with Dr Simic, I felt free to encounter the truth. I began questioning the doctor closely; I wanted the facts, the possibilities, the prognosis. And Dr Simic patiently answered my questions, giving me honest answers and not trying to shield me from the darker consequences of the accident. As the serious implications began to dawn on me, I was conscious of a need to handle them by myself, without Ron. There would be time enough for me to be concerned with his pain—right now I had to deal with my own feelings. We talked for a long time.

'I want to know what the X-rays showed.'

'Well, there is a crack in your third vertebra. That in itself is not too serious—time will mend that. Indeed, if it were the only damage, the brace might have done some good.'

'But the real problem?'

'Yes—you must understand, Nancy, how your

36

'spine works. The vertebrae are piled up in a column, and down the centre runs the spinal cord, carrying all the nerve impulses, all the messages to your brain. Your fourth and fifth vertebrae have become misplaced. They overlap, but they are not sitting one on top of the other any more. Here, let me show you.'

He grabbed Ron's letter-writing pad and tore out a page, and sketched for me a column of short horizontal lines.

'These are the vertebrae—their shape is really much more complicated, but never mind. In between, cushioning them, the discs. So, we have flexibility, we bend and stretch, not rigid, see? Down the centre, that important spinal cord.'

Down through the pile of lines he drew one long vertical. Then, with a sudden movement, he tore the paper in half, across his long line, and between two of the short lines.

'If the spinal cord is severed—that is the end. No more messages, no more movement—ever.'

'That isn't what has happened to me, is it?' I asked hesitantly.

'No, Nancy, you have been lucky.' He looked at my swollen face and my inert body, and smiled gently. 'Yes, lucky—perhaps.'

Carefully he fitted his two pieces of paper together again, but slightly off-centre.

'The cord is not severed—but it is trapped, you see, because these two vertebrae are no longer aligned. There is great pressure on it, so no messages are getting through. That is why you have no sensation below your shoulders. Above the fracture, you see, everything is working. Now, what we have to do is to stretch your whole spine, so there is no pressure on the cord. And then, we hope, those two vertebrae will slip back into position.'

'Will they go right back?' I asked eagerly.

'I think that is very unlikely, Nancy. When you get to England they will be able to tell you more.'

'How will they stretch the spine?'

'The operation will be the same as we use here. We drill holes in the skull—here and here.' He pointed just above his temples. 'We insert metal rods to hold the apparatus. Then we attach weights behind your head to pull upwards, and we tilt the bed so that gravity will pull the body down. In England they have other ways of doing that—and they have Stryker frames, so you can be turned over, front to back, easily. Then they monitor the process of realignment. When it stops—that is as far as they can go to help you.'

'Suppose it goes—say, reasonably well.' I didn't want to be over-optimistic. 'Will I be able to walk?'

'That is only a possibility. It is more likely that you will be in a wheelchair.'

'What about children? Will I be able to have children?'

'Again, I cannot say definitely. So much depends on the degree of permanent damage. There is a slight possibility—but I should not want you to rely on it. No one cay say yet. Do not raise your hopes.'

'I'm not hoping for anything, doctor. Just trying to find out—the best and the worst.'

Just then the door opened, and Ron came in. One looked at his downcast face and drooping shoulders told me what I wanted to know.

'No flights?'

'I'm sorry, Nan. I've been to the British and American embassies. We've missed a BEA flight by twenty minutes. There's nothing else for two days.'

'Oh, that's great!' I exclaimed. 'I'm sorry, Ron, but I just couldn't face being moved again. I'd much rather have Dr Simic do the operation.'

Dr Simic looked from Ron's anxious face to my delighted one. The skin on my face was by now taut and shiny with the swelling, but I was managing to smile. He made up his mind.

'I will make arrangements for the operation. We will do it this evening, as soon as the theatre is free. The nurses will come this afternoon to get you ready, Nancy.' And he left.

He hadn't told me, however, what 'getting ready' entailed. I looked aghast as the two nurses came in with scissors and an electric razor, and I burst into tears.

'Not my hair—oh, please—not my hair!'

Ron was almost amused. 'I don't know, Nancy. You're lying there with a broken neck, and you're crying because you've got to have your hair cut off!'

'Oh, please—I can't be bald! Can't you leave me some?' I had been so proud of my long hair; somehow it seemed to be the final humiliation to be shaved as well as naked and helpless. In the end the nurses took pity on me and compromised: they shaved the sides of my head and left me a strip of long hair over the centre of my head, like a Mohican. It looked, probably, even odder than being completely bald, but it could at least be spread out over my head to cover it. I hadn't seen myself in a mirror, or I would have been so horrified by the sight of my face that baldness might have seemed a minor problem.

Nevertheless, I wept all that afternoon—not just

39

over the loss of my hair, but like Ron earlier, for the whole overturning of our lives.

I thought about spending the rest of my life in a wheelchair—childless, helpless, dependent on Ron. I was struck by a terrible thought—suppose the accident had happened before our marriage? Would we still have got married? Would I have imposed on Ron the burden of a wife confined to a wheelchair? I knew quite well that it's pointless to play the 'what if...' game with God, but I was haunted by this thought. How could both facts—our marriage and the accident—be part of God's plan for us? If God really intended me to live as a helpless invalid, had I been wrong in thinking that it was his plan that I should be a missionary and marry Ron?

I thought of our life in Iran: the first time I watched a baby being born, at a hospital in Tehran; the time we visited a mullah's home and ate rice and khoresh with his family; the times we stood and watched Persian carpets being run over by Tehran traffic, to deepen the intricate pattern and increase their value; the times I'd bargained at the market stalls for fruit and cooking oil; the time I'd spent teaching English to a small class of girls at a local school. We both enjoyed something of a pioneer lifestyle and that year we'd immersed ourselves in the language and culture, attending weddings, funerals, concerts and plays. While Ron travelled to the provinces visiting the scattered Christian churches, taking books and Bibles to encourage them, I taught English and visited homes daily with a friend. We'd just completed a summer of tremendous work and excitement, when forty young Iranians had joined us to declare their Christian faith. I simply couldn't imagine any other sort of life!

I'd always had an independent, headstrong nature.

My parents recognised this, and long before any thought of marriage had entered my head, my mother had been praying about my future husband. 'A man of God,' she'd said firmly, 'because only someone with authority will be able to guide and control Nan.'

I knew that in Ron I had found a man of God, intent on doing the Father's will, and I wanted to go with him and work alongside him in everything. Marrying Ron had been one of the most important decisions of my life. Following Christ had been the other. I refused to believe that I had been wrong in either case. I was committed to my life as a missionary for Christ, and to sharing my life with Ron—helping him, not dragging him down. I decided that whatever the consequences of the operation—even if I were confined to a wheelchair—I would continue with both these things. After all, I argued to myself, within missionary work I would have the help of the other team members, so I need not be a burden to Ron. Somehow I would go on doing the task that God had given me. When the nurses came at seven o'clock to give the pre-med, I had stopped crying. But I still regretted my hair.

They wouldn't let Ron stay with me in the operating theatre, so he waited while I was transferred from the trolley to the operating table, and then went to wait in the corridor outside. Dr Simic leaned over me.

'Nancy, I have a colleague here to help me. He speaks a little English, so we will all understand you. You are not going to sleep, you know. We will give you an anaesthetic in your head, so you will feel no pain, but you must talk to us and answer our questions. Then we can be sure you are all right, yes?'

I offered the new doctor the tight-lipped grimace

that passed for a smile on my swollen face. 'How long will it take?'

'About an hour. Imagine you are in the dentist's chair—it is just like drilling an upper tooth.'

The doctors went off to get ready, and I lay still, waiting for someone to come with the local anaesthetic. The theatre lights above the table were very bright, and I closed my eyes to shield them from the glare. I wondered if I would really come through this operation. Perhaps I was simply going to die. The table was hard, and I felt the uselessness of my limbs as though I were pinned to it, hand and foot. Then I opened my eyes and I saw, very clearly, just beyond the blinding lights, the shape of the cross. I thought, just as I had at the moment of the accident, Is this it? Is this my time to die? The answer came instantly into my mind, as clearly as if a voice had spoken, 'Not you, Nancy, but I. I died for you. I was nailed to a cross— do you mind being fastened to a table? I came through death for you. I live, and you will live.' For the first time, the cross of Christ became a practical reality for me. The Bible verse I had adopted long ago as my life's ambition stirred in my memory: 'I eagerly expect and hope that I will in no way be ashamed, but will have sufficient courage so that now as always Christ will be exalted in my body, whether by life or death. For to me, to live is Christ and to die is gain.' (Phil 1:20, 21).

I'm not ordinarily given to visions, but I was sure that these words of the apostle Paul were meant for me in my moment of need. Christ had already faced the sting of death for me, and I relaxed in that knowledge.

Then the anaesthetist came and gave me two injections, one on either side of my face. There was another pause while my face went numb—Dr Simic was right, it was just like the dentist's anaesthetic—then the doctors returned.

'OK, Nancy, we will begin drilling. Are you ready?'

'Sure, doctor.'

The drill started up. It seemed to go on for ever, a dull grinding sound which made my whole head vibrate. Someone was holding my face still, and there arose a sickening smoky smell—the stench of bone burning in the heat generated by the drill. The doctors talked to me all the time, though the huge dose of local anaesthetic made me rather vague and wandering in my replies.

'Doctor, I can see it!'

'See what, Nancy?'

'I can see the drill, it's come through behind my eyes!'

Outside, Ron could hear gales of laughter from the doctors at the silly things I was saying, and he paced up and down in anger. How could they laugh?

At last the drilling stopped for a moment.

'Have you finished?' I found I was shouting into the sudden silence.

'It won't be long, Nancy. We're going round to start on the other side.' And the grinding and the vibration began again. It took a long time because the task required absolute precision—once the pins were inserted in my skull they had to stay there without any movement. Eventually they finished, though my head went on ringing for hours. Once the metal rods were fixed in the holes, weights were threaded on to a wire which ran over the head of the bed. Then the bed was tilted at precisely the right angle to achieve the required traction.

Only then was Ron allowed to come in. The operating theatre looked like a battlefield: the walls were spattered with blood. The first incisions had released the pressure under my skin, and the accumulated blood had shot out across the room. My face was still black and bruised, I was strung with pulleys and weights, and I was exhausted. Gently Ron stroked my face.

'Nan,' he said soberly, 'you look beautiful.'

Chapter 3

During the weeks that followed I was aware of a strange emptiness; it was a hiatus, a period of waiting for the treatment to begin to take effect. Privately I questioned God: 'Lord, what if I never walk again? How can I be of any use to you? Why didn't I die?' I almost felt disappointed. I didn't tell Ron of my thoughts, for I didn't want to discourage him.

During this period the quietness of prayer became increasingly important to me: it reminded me of my dependence on God. I thought back to my happy and secure childhood, and smiled wryly to recall how anxious I'd been to leave home behind me. My parents couldn't afford to put any of their children through college, so I always knew I would have to work to earn enough money to go to the Moody Bible Institute, which was my aim. So eager was I to try my wings and leave the nest that as soon as I graduated from High School I travelled some 500 miles to Denver, Colorado, to work. Independence was my immediate goal: I wanted to make my own way in life, to get to know and like myself with no help from my family, to survive life alone with only the help of my Heavenly Father.

Independence. As I reflected on how hastily I'd abandoned family life, my thoughts clouded with despair. It had seemed so easy then. I always hated asking for help; coming from a family where teamwork was essential, where each member carried responsibility without question, I was used to doing things without interference. Now my whole being rebelled against the impossible position in which I found myself. How on earth was I to cope and remain sane? 'Lord,' I prayed, 'why didn't you take me home after all? What good am I to myself, to Ron, to you, to anyone? Surely you didn't expect me to give up my independence? To let other people look after me for the rest of my life?'

I felt as though a tornado had struck my passive brain. Images of the future crowded in, and they were all dark ones: the isolation of being confined to a wheelchair, unable to walk or run or even stand up; constantly having to summon help for my most basic needs—eating, washing, dressing; Ron reduced to a nursemaid, having to deal with catheters and bedpans. I shuddered and closed my eyes, but there was no escape from my thoughts. I couldn't even cry much, because someone else had to wipe my nose and eyes for me. Ron had enough grief without taking on mine, I felt. Once, as I was talking with Dr Simic, depression overwhelmed me and I wept uncontrollably. He let me cry, holding my fevered cheeks with his firm strong hands and catching the streams of tears with paper handkerchiefs. He reasoned that he was constantly learning from disabled patients, from their despair as well as their positive will. Handicapped people need to come to terms with themselves and the way they affect others, he said. I could bring sorrow and hurt to my situation or—if I chose—enjoyment and help. His calm frankness restored my humour, as he fumbled around looking for a wetted towel to soothe my swollen eyes.

After my outburst I felt better, as though my tears had released a hard knot of tension inside me. And after all, we couldn't know exactly what my condition would be until the treatment had taken effect. It was foolish to worry about tomorrow. I closed my eyes and determined to practise that Bible verse I had learned as a child: 'I have the strength to face all conditions by the power Christ gives me' (Phil 4:13 GNB).

Around this time word had reached home of what had happened, and my closest friend, Drena Verwer, had met for prayer with other friends from OM. 'Lord,' they had prayed, 'either take Nan home and enjoy her now, or let her walk again. You know she's a runner and loves action.' I found it hard to contemplate any form of life which didn't include activity (preferably of the frenetic and enthusiastic variety which was my hallmark!) yet I knew that I had to search for God's will for me, whatever it might be. I concluded that as God had not taken me at the crisis, then he must intend me to live. I felt as though I should have died in the accident, and again on the operating table; therefore whatever followed was a kind of resurrection. I was sure that God wanted me renewed to live, as Christ was. Although Christ came through death perfect, and I had missed death and emerged damaged and disabled, nevertheless I should live as he intended; I should be the best that I could be.

During those early waiting days after the operation, as I lay and endured the discomfort of traction, I swung from despair to hope and back again. Yet all the while this conviction was growing in me, that God could use me somehow, and that I was saved for some purpose. 'In fact God has arranged the parts in the body, every one of them, just as he wanted them to be...Now you are the body of Christ, and each one of you is a part of it' (1 Cor 12:18, 27).

I understood, now, how vital the spine is to the overall function of the body. The centre of the whole nervous system is encased in these small vertebrae: pressure on any part of the spine causes pain and malfunction. In the end, all my thinking, Ron's reading aloud of the Bible, and our praying together, seemed to come down to this: God was saying to me,

'You may not ever be the mouthpiece, the feet to go or the hands to do. But you can still be a source of power, if you are prepared to take your proper place of prayer. You can be the spine in the Body of Christ, the nerve centre for more active members. You must learn to work in partnership to do my will.'

I wrestled with the idea. Was I to place myself in the background—unseen, unnoticed, but vital? Was I willing to take this role, in silence, and let others fulfil my dreams? The very thought filled me with restless energy, for I loved action. I'd said I was willing to go anywhere, do anything in the Lord's service—but I wasn't willing to do nothing. For sure, God had work to do to change my stubborn heart.

Meanwhile, as I was trying to come to terms with all this, my days were not empty. Ron was in regular contact with the American and British embassies after their failure to arrange suitable flights home for us, and they kindly loaned us books from their libraries. Ron had to read aloud—even if it had been possible to prop a book open for me, I couldn't read because the rods in my head made it impossible for me to wear my glasses. (When, months later, the rods were finally removed and I could wear them again, the world swam into focus and life immediately became much more interesting!)

Together we studied Serbo-Croat, to make communication with other patients and the nurses easier; we read the Don Camillo books of Giovanni Guareschi, and thrillers by Alistair MacLean. We set ourselves goals, to read and discuss books on American history or to study certain passages of the Bible. One day, as Ron was reading aloud from the second book of Samuel, we came to the story of David and Bathsheba, and how the prophet Nathan bravely rebuked the king for his evil deeds.

'That's it!' cried Ron. 'I really like Nathan. He had the nerve not to bow and scrape to the king, he had the guts to show David his error. That's what we'll call our first son—Nathan!'

'But, Ron,' I protested, 'you know what the doctor said. We may not be able to have any children...'

Ron was adamant, however, so I let it pass. But he seemed to be very confident for the future.

Our reading was constantly interrupted by the nurses who came to turn me. Because of the pressure sores I already had, I was forced to spend all my time on my sides, to allow them to heal. I could spend about one and a half hours on my left side, and about two hours on my right, and so at those intervals, day and night, I had to be turned. This task took three nurses, one at my head, one at my waist, and one at my ankles. The movement had to be carefully synchronised, and was most comfortable when it was done by three nurses who were used to working together, but often Ron had to help. In spite of our pleas, the nurses (all men) were often smoking. On several occasions cigarette ash fell on to my naked body, and Ron had to watch out for this, since I couldn't feel if I was burned.

At intervals the sores on my head and bottom were dressed. The putrefying flesh had to be scooped out, and the smell was awful. The one on my bottom was about two inches in diameter and very deep: in the end they had excavated a deep cone, and the doctors considered that a skin graft might be the only way of achieving full healing. In fact it did eventually heal, though I still have a large indentation there. The sore on the back of my head was not so severe, but worse from one point of view—being above my shoulders, it was in the area where I still had feeling, and the dressing of it was very painful. It, too, eventually healed, though the scar remains bald and I have to be very careful about how I arrange my hair to hide it.

I soon became used to the traction: I was lying in an ordinary hospital bed, which was somehow arranged to slant so that my own body weight of around 135 lbs was pulling against the weights of 18 lbs hanging over the top of the bed, and suspended from the calliper arrangement fixed to my head. One day a visitor was talking animatedly to Ron, and I had some difficulty in breaking into their conversation to tell her that her small son was behind the bed, trying to swing on the weights!

Meanwhile, the physiotherapist came daily to work with me. He was blind, and I soon learned to respect his dedication. Ron's confidence was infectious: I was gradually becoming assured that there was a possibility of improvement, but that I would have to fight for whatever quality of life I was to attain. Elech, the physiotherapist, manipulated each part of me, each finger, wrist and hand, working on up my arms, biceps and triceps, then feet and legs. He tested each area for feeling with cotton wool and pins, and gradually I began to feel tired and bruised and sore after each session.

Then, one day, as Elech was moving my right arm, encouraging me to try to resist his movements by grunting 'Pool' and 'Poosh', suddenly there was a twitch in the muscle—I was moving my arm! The movements were clumsy and wild, but gradually strength began to appear in the muscles that had lain lifeless for so long. At first I could control only my arm—I was still unable to move my fingers—but then similar gross control began to appear in my right leg. Although the physiotherapy exhausted me, I found the beginnings of restoration exciting, and attacked each session with enthusiasm. At last, something was happening; my healing was beginning!

It was several days more before I began to have some movement in my fingers, and just opening and closing a fist was a challenge: I had to concentrate immensely hard to will those fingers to move. I felt as though my brain were a lighthouse sending out a beam on a foggy night—sometimes the message penetrated the fog, but sometimes it got smothered on the way.

My first goal was to scratch my own nose and learn to feed myself with the minimum help: it took about four weeks of hard and determined work before I succeeded, but what a day that was. Managing to grasp a spoon was a major achievement. Ron and I would be in peals of laughter for my aim, to begin with, was poor, and a spoonful of food was just as likely to end up on my forehead as in my mouth. Gradually this improved, as did my strength—to begin with, just lifting an apple seemed to be a colossal effort—but there were problems. For one thing, all this improvement was confined to the right side; there was no sign of movement on the left side of my body. The progress seemed agonisingly slow, and I was bored with hearing Elech's repeated question, 'You feel this?' as he worked on my skin with pins.

At last I began to respond—on my left side I could feel heat and cold, the touch of the sheet, and finally that insistent pricking of the pins; yet still there was no movement there. The right side showed promise of strength, and my co-ordination was improving daily, yet there I had no sensory awareness at all. It was hard to hold a cup when I could not feel it, and frustrating to feel things with the other hand which I was quite unable to move. I really didn't know whether to feel optimistic or not, so I just went on doggedly with the everlasting physiotherapy.

After about six weeks of this, Ron received a telephone call from an OM conference in Belgium.

'We're having a day of prayer,' our friend Jonathan told him. 'Give us something specific to claim for Nan.'

After a brief pause Ron responded, 'Ask God for movement in her left leg.'

Unaware of this conversation, I was beginning yet another day of hospital routine: the nurses dressed my head wounds and bedsores, the cleaning lady clattered about the room sweeping and mopping, and I waited for Ron to come back from his daily walk to the Embassy for the post and the library books. Idly, I tightened my muscles as I had been taught, tried to move my left heel—and cried out aloud.

'Hey! I moved!'

Hardly daring to believe it, I lay there impatiently

waiting for Ron to return. I didn't try it again—I wanted to conserve my strength!

As soon as he walked through the door, I called, 'Honey, guess what?'

'What happened?' he asked, hurrying to the side of the bed.

'Look,' I answered, 'pull my leg straight.'

He lifted the sheet and straightened my leg. With an enormous effort I managed to pull my left leg along the bed about two inches.

'Praise the Lord!' he cried. 'That's what Jonathan's been praying for!'

Then he told me the whole story of the phone call and the two hundred young people in Belgium praying for me.

That afternoon the duty doctor made his rounds with the medical students, and I told him about the first movement in my leg, insisting that he translate for me, sentence by sentence, as I told them how God was answering prayer.

That first leg movement really spurred me on to greater efforts, because for the first time it began to look as though there was a possibility of regaining movement in my whole body—and that meant that I might walk again. The daily physiotherapy sessions became sweat-shops as I got used to pulling that leg a little further each day, and watched eagerly for life elsewhere. Only a couple of days later I found I had twitching movements in my left arm, and the process began again. In each case, the extremities—the fingers and toes—were the last to co-operate.

After the first four weeks of traction, when the routine of physiotherapy and pin-pricking had been established, Dr Simic explained to me that he wanted to administer a 'drug cocktail'. This cocktail was a mixture of muscle relaxants and other drugs, designed to enhance the effects of the traction by relaxing every muscle completely. The drugs were delivered from a drip-feed bottle into my arm, and Dr Simic himself monitored the process which took three or four hours. He prepared us for the experience well in advance, and the first session took place on a Friday night, after his usual duties were over. I watched the level in the drip bottle falling slowly as the drugs were fed into my arm, and dozed in and out of sleep as every muscle and nerve relaxed. Ron and Dr Simic talked on many subjects during these hours, about Yugoslavian history, about the influence of Communism, about the Orthodox Church and Christianity, and what the apostle Paul has to say about love and marriage. I marvelled at the doctor's wealth of knowledge and culture, at the patience with which he listened to our point of view, and the interest he evinced in Ron's explanations of the gospel message.

The drugs were given three times, at two-week intervals. During the third session, as Ron and the doctor were talking, I thought I felt a kind of twitching in my neck, but assumed that I was imagining things. However, on the following morning I was X-rayed, and the results showed that the displaced vertebra had indeed moved closer to alignment with the others.

While all these exciting developments were taking place we became more and more accustomed to the life of the hospital. At first there were just the two of us in our small room, but after a few weeks a nurse asked us if we would mind sharing our room with an eighteen-year-old English boy called David.

David had a severe spinal injury from a diving

accident, and had had a tracheotomy to enable him to breathe. This meant that he was unable to speak unless someone closed the hole in his throat, so that the air could pass over his vocal cords. When he arrived he was accompanied by his friend Alf, who was in despair about his accident. It soon became clear that they had been placed with us not only because of our common language, but so that Ron could coach Alf, and teach him how to help nurse David. Ron's tireless work with me had forced him to become something of an expert, and he certainly saved the nursing staff an immense amount of work. David and Alf were with us for only four days, but during that time Ron was able to help them a great deal, not only physically but spiritually.

David, like me, had been very close to death, and he knew it. He knew also that his injuries were more severe than mine, and that he would be quadriplegic, totally dependent on others for everything. When he wanted to speak to us, he would make a clicking sound with his tongue, so that Ron or Alf would come and place a finger over the hole in his throat. One day he clicked for Ron to come to him.

'Ron,' he said, with difficulty, 'do you reckon I'm going to die?'

'I don't know, David,' Ron replied. 'The doctor says you're stable enough to travel back to England soon, doesn't he? The main thing is, are you ready to meet your Creator?'

'What?' asked David. 'What do you mean?'

'Well, you know the condition you're in. You have now to put your life in someone else's hands—just as Nan has had to depend on other people for everything.'

'Don't look at me,' I broke in. 'Don't use me as an

example.' At this point I was beginning to regain some movement, and I felt that I was seeing miracles happen, but I knew only too well the danger of raising false hopes. My recovery, if it happened, would be based on faith, medical co-operation and prayer, but I didn't want David to think we were dangling the carrot of healing before him.

'OK,' said David. 'But I know I shall be disabled for ever now. What else is there to say?'

'Well,' responded Ron. 'Don't you want someone more capable even than the doctors to look after your life?'

David eyed him curiously. 'Who's that?' he asked.

'I can give you my friend,' said Ron. 'Jesus Christ. He doesn't offer just hope for healing. If you come to him and trust him to look after you, then it really doesn't matter whether you live or die. If you die, you will be home with him. If you live, then your life will be more meaningful because he will be with you. Isn't that what you want?'

David was thoughtful for some time. Ron took his hand away from David's throat, meaning to leave him to think all this over, but at once David clicked urgently with his tongue.

'Yes, I do,' he said. 'How do I do it?'

I lay and listened as Ron led David in that first halting prayer of commitment, and silently thanked God.

Ron was excited at the prospect of so many growing relationships in the hospital environment. Whenever a visitor came to my room to talk to me, or if I was having treatment in which he was not needed, Ron would go off around the wards in search of people to talk to. Sometimes he would wheel my bed around the wards so that I could meet some of his new friends (and see that their plight was often worse than mine). He got OM to send him Bible portions in Serbo-Croat, which he distributed to patients, and as our grasp of the language grew, we talked to people about Jesus—all this in a state hospital in a Communist country! At first I was concerned that the doctors would disapprove of his activities and would send him away, but he was far too useful around the hospital, helping the nurses, nursing me, and always willing to help anyone. I stopped worrying about this one day when I saw Dr Simic come into the room. He had deep trouser turn-ups, and in one of these he carried a small New Testament that Ron had given him. I decided that if things had gone that far, and the head of the department was openly reading the gospel, it wasn't likely that Ron's other activities would land us in trouble.

Then another worry took its place. After David had left us to travel back to a hospital in Cardiff, the nurses found a replacement room-mate for me. She was a German woman who was married to a Palestinian husband. They had been involved in a horrific car crash in which she was very severely injured, but he had emerged unscathed. They stayed together in our room, and I suppose the idea was that he would help nurse his wife as Ron helped to nurse me. However, Mohammed had a different outlook on life; a happy, easy-going fellow, he filled the room with friends and acquaintances, who talked, laughed and smoked all day long. It was like living in a continual party, and desperate though I became for some peace and quiet, I felt even sorrier for his wife. Like David, she had had a tracheotomy, and was unable to talk unless someone helped her (which her husband could seldom be bothered to do). In any case, she spoke little English. Because I was on the other side of the room and immobile, we couldn't converse.

Mohammed was a big, burly, curly-haired man, used to partying and the high life, and when he bothered to talk to his wife it was with a nonchalant attitude.

'Of course we'll go dancing again, we'll travel and do things,' he would say, when it was quite obvious that she would be disabled for the rest of her life. I must confess that I hated him for giving her false hopes, perhaps the worst torture of all.

Ron was less irritated by them than I was, partly perhaps because he was able to escape from the noise, the smoke, and the sight of their belongings and dirty washing strewn all over the room. He went out of his way to try to be kind and helpful to them. Then one evening he returned from his trip to the embassy, absolutely furious. He had passed Mohammed outside the hospital, sitting on a park bench with a woman with whom he was evidently on very intimate terms.

We had both spent time in Iran studying Muslim culture and religion, and I knew Mohammed's likely attitude to us, so I urged Ron to be careful and to say nothing which might annoy him. Ron felt that the only way he could deal with his own anger was to show care for Mohammed. He waited until everyone else was asleep, then he gathered up all Mohammed's dirty socks, filled a basin with soapy water and washed them, draping them over a radiator to dry.

Soon afterwards the couple flew to Beirut for further treatment, but I often thought about that poor woman and the likely future for her marriage. By contrast, I felt most fortunate: I had a devoted husband who loved me and nursed me with care; I had a loving Heavenly Father who answered prayer; and I had a family and friends who were praying for me. In spite of my desperate condition, I realised the practicality of Paul's words: 'Godliness with contentment is great gain' (1 Tim 6:6).

Chapter 4

Dr Simic came into my room brandishing yet another set of X-ray pictures.

'Good news, Nancy,' he cried. 'That last drug cocktail has done the trick. The vertebra has slipped back almost into alignment!'

'That's great,' I replied. 'What happens now?'

'Well, your traction has worked, so we can take off all these bits of metal and set you free!'

Dr Simic was evidently feeling very pleased with himself, so I tried to look excited, too. But inwardly I was aware of a strange hesitancy, and I was puzzled by my reaction. After all, this was what we had been working so hard for, all these weeks. Admittedly, I was still more than a little unbalanced in my abilities. On my left side I was regaining some feeling—hot and cold, smooth and rough textures, and I could even detect the location of some of the pinpricks—and slow, clumsy movement was beginning. On the right side of my entire body I still had no sensation at all, but the movement was getting much more distinct and my strength was increasing daily. Still, I was far from independent, and I realised that the metal rods and weights felt to me like an anchor, holding me safely pinned to the bed. The thought of being without them frightened me. Suppose I fell off the bed? Suppose the nurses dropped me when they were turning me? Ron tried to reassure me, but after weeks of invariable hospital routine, in which I felt safe, my fears of even this small change grew out of all proportion to the difference it would really make.

When the great day came I was taken back to the operating theatre. The removal was painful, and I screamed as the doctors unhooked the weights and gently slid the rods out of the holes in my skull. I felt, literally, light-headed for a moment, and then I was filled with elation.

The last time I had been in that theatre I had been shocked, totally paralysed, with festering wounds and a blackened face. Now, only a few weeks later, I was being healed! My wounds had scabbed, the septic places were clean, my face had been restored to its normal colour and shape, and even my hair was beginning to grow back. But most of all, I was beginning to move: once the traction was gone I was free— free to learn once again to take possession of my body, to regain my independence. At that moment I resolved that whatever the doctors said, I would go one better: I would walk again, I would bear children, I would live a real life—my life. My excitement overrode the pain, and the next step to freedom permeated my thoughts all that day.

I began to move about more in the bed—squirming instead of lying passive and still. I still needed help in turning onto my sides, and my back was supported by pillows. I imagined what it would be like to sit up for the first time, to look out of a window or peer down a hallway. The ceiling and walls became increasingly boring. Now at last I was sure that I would not be confined to a bed indefinitely—it might take a while to run, but walk I must...

At the onset of the treatment, Dr Simic had assured us that he would realign the vertebra if that were at all possible. However, he had never had any illusions about the process of rehabilitation: for that we must return to England. Accordingly, as I continued to progress, he helped Ron to write letters to various English hospitals, outlining my case and the kind of treatment I would need. It seemed no time at all before they had made all the arrangements. In December, Stanmore Orthopaedic Hospital in Middlesex wrote back positively, assigning me to one of their consultants, booking a bed for me, and offering to manage the transfer from the plane to the airport and on to Stanmore.

Although I was glad to be released, that parting from our 'camp-site' in the hospital was an enormous step: saying goodbye to everyone was an ordeal that took a week. It was extraordinary how many people we had met in those three months. Ron wheeled my bed from ward to ward so that I could speak to special friends, so many of whom were desperately ill or severely disabled. I wanted to say to everyone,

'Take heart; look at me: I'm a Humpty Dumpty who has been put together! Your doctors and nurses have restored me from a splodge of crumpled flesh to the beginning of a new life.' And to a few, who had shared something deeper of my healing, I could say, 'These cracks will heal. I will walk again, and with God's help I will be his showpiece. The Lord is honoured by life or by death, but he allowed me to live, and I know that he'll teach me to cope with my life fulfillingly.'

We had no words with which to thank Dr Simic

and his staff, though they knew the extent of our gratitude. When at last I saw Ron signing me out, and my care was officially handed over from Dr Simic, I wept as he shook our hands and kissed me goodbye.

'We'll never forget you,' I told him. 'Goodbye.'

As it happened, my final words were a little premature: what I had forgotten was the particular brand of efficiency in the Belgrade hospital. I was placed on a canvas stretcher supported by two wooden poles, and laid to rest on the floor in the hallway. And there we stayed for almost an hour. It was freezing, and although we tried to keep cheerful, I grew grumpier and more concerned as we grew colder. 'Goodbye' seemed rather too abrupt a word for such a long-drawn-out parting.

At last I heard footsteps along the corridor and a face appeared above me. I was introduced to the lady doctor who was to be responsible for my transfer to the airport, and she organised two nurses to carry me to the ambulance. We were relieved to be on the move at last, and I was excited at the thought: it would be the first time for three months that I had been outside the hospital.

'This is it,' I said to Ron as the ambulance drew up at the airport, 'back to the real world.'

We were ushered into a small room, where my canvas stretcher was placed on the floor again, and I lay there while Ron and the doctor went off to sort out the arrangements and the boarding tickets: we had had to pay for six seats on the aircraft, which were removed from the rear of the plane so that my stretcher could be inserted. The floor was hard, I was covered only by a thin blanket, and it was already two hours since I had last been turned, but I tried to ignore the discomfort, telling myself that I would soon be on my way to England.

After some time two airline stewards arrived, and they lifted my stretcher, rather inexpertly, and took me out to the plane where Ron and the doctor were waiting. They carried me up the steps through the luggage hold—the only opening wide enough for the stretcher—and I was just planning some joking remark to greet Ron, about being handled like a piece of luggage, when one side of the stretcher collapsed, and I was dropped onto the floor.

Pandemonium broke loose: one of the stewards yelled, and the doctor began to shout hysterically; Ron was trying to fight his way through the people to get to me as I was attempting to explain to the stewards (who spoke little English) how best to right the stretcher.

'It's OK, Ron,' I said, as he arrived at my feet. 'I'm not hurt: I fell on my right side and my neck hasn't been jolted. Just sort out the stretcher, will you? And please, calm down that doctor!' The doctor wasn't really a great deal of help, standing crying in a corner, so Ron organised the move into the seats, where I was strapped in tightly, reassured the doctor that we would not be making any complaints or reports about her, and saw her thankfully off the plane.

'And that,' he said as he strapped himself into his seat, 'is the end of Yugoslavian health care. I'll be glad to get you safely to England, Nan. I know Dr Simic was wonderful, but you wait till you get inside an English hospital; then I'll relax.'

It was an uneventful trip, though I found the sensations very peculiar. The seats had been removed in a line so that my feet pointed towards the front of the plane: the result was that the take-off stood me on my head, and the landing made all the blood rush to my feet. My circulation had been accustomed to operating entirely in a horizontal position for such a long while that I almost fainted, but fortunately it didn't last for long.

During the flight I was very quiet and subdued, refusing food from the stewardess and trying to avoid attention. I felt very exposed, encountering the real world for the first time. I was no longer surrounded by other sick or injured people, and I was aware of many curious stares from the other passengers. Only my shorn head showed above the blankets, with its single strip of longer hair like a mohican: one man asked Ron if I was his brother! I wondered if Ron spent all his time explaining me and my accident.

The other reason for my quiet mood was that I was worried about disembarking. Being dropped had been frightening, although I kept calm at the time. I could so easily have been seriously injured, and undone all the hard and painful work of the last months. I felt helpless and dependent again, and insecure now that I was left to the care of the non-medical airline staff. So much could go wrong—and how would they ever get me off this plane?

I need not have worried; the aircraft taxied to a halt on the runway at Heathrow, and even before the drone of the engines had faded I heard a strident voice dominating the hubbub around me.

'I have a patient on this plane—where's my patient? I must come on board.'

How she had managed it I do not know, but the sister from Stanmore Hospital must have been waiting on the runway, and she appeared on board as soon as a door was opened. I was unable to believe the expertise with which my removal was effected: before any-

one else made a move I was transferred to a comfortable sling stretcher and hoisted back through the luggage hold into the fresh, damp air of an English night.
In no time, it seemed, I was lying on a wheeled trolley
between crisp clean sheets, placed in an ambulance
with the sister and whisked away to a quiet, warm
medical room at the airport. Within half an hour all
the official papers were completed and the sister went
to telephone the hospital that we were on our way. I
looked at the door as it closed behind her.

'I never saw anything like that in my life,' I said to
Ron. 'What an amazing lady! I believe she'd have
bullied the pilot if necessary!'

'I told you so,' said Ron smugly. 'You'll be well
looked after now.'

We arrived at Stanmore Hospital just before midnight
and the night sister checked me into the ward. I was
back in the familiar hospital environment, yet with a
difference—at one end of the long ward was the night
sister's desk, with a low light burning. Everything was
quiet, warm and clean, and I felt immensely reassured
that I was indeed in good hands.

I was so busy looking around at my new surroundings that I'd almost forgotten that Ron had to leave.

'I'll have to go now, Nan, or I'll miss the last train,'
he said. He was going to Chelsfield, in Kent, to stay
with his aunt and uncle.

'Oh, Ron, don't go yet,' I pleaded. 'Don't leave me
tonight.'

'I can't stay here as I did in Belgrade,' he replied.
'There are twenty-one other women in this ward, for a
start! And you don't need me now—you're safe here.'
He took my left hand in his, so that I could feel his
touch. 'It's Friday night. You need a couple of days to

yourself, to get settled. I'll come and visit you as soon as I can, but I must leave you in their care over the weekend.'

The truth was that I simply could not imagine myself kissing him goodnight and goodbye, after he had been my shadow for ninety-three days and nights.

I slept restlessly in the strange bed, and was utterly confused to be awoken at 5.30 am by an orderly bringing me a cup of tea. I would have preferred coffee to tea, and more sleep to either, but the cosy English voice reconciled me to being awake, and the kindly orderlies seemed shocked at the idea that anyone should refuse such an essential part of the routine. Warm water was brought for washing, and the night staff did a round of temperature-taking and medication before going off duty. I soon learned that unlike Belgrade, where such arrangements were haphazard to say the least, at Stanmore the routines of breakfast, bed-making and cleaning worked like clockwork.

Two male orderlies arrived at my bedside with a stretcher on wheels.

'We're taking you to be X-rayed this morning, Nancy,' said the sister briskly. 'We want pictures so we can see just how much healing has occurred.'

Every movement was decisive as the two men lifted me on to the trolley and wheeled me out of the ward and along a covered walkway in the open air. It was my first time out in the open in daylight, and the cool damp air tasted delightful as I drew in deep breaths.

The porters took me through several sets of doors and parked me in a corridor in the X-ray department. Doctors and nurses hurried by, but I wasn't left alone for long. A young nurse holding a slip of paper in her hand approached me, and smiled encouragingly. Slowly and deliberately she asked,

'Do—you—speak—English?'

'Yes,' I replied with a grin, 'quite well.'

She looked down at her paper in surprise. 'Haven't you just arrived from Yugoslavia?'

'Well, yes,' I explained, 'but I'm an American married to an Englishman.'

She broke into a laugh. 'Well, that's a relief. I thought I was going to have awful trouble explaining X-rays to you.' She wheeled me off to the radiography department.

I was rolled into every imaginable position, and after an hour or so and what seemed like dozens of X-rays, I was exhausted. It was comforting to return to the ward and see my bed all made up and waiting.

'Just in time, dear, for some Levensees,' said a nurse. I looked at her blankly, totally bemused—was it the name of a hospital routine or an English drink? It turned out to be 'elevenses', a custom unfamiliar to me, as was the strange milky coffee I was offered. I was reminded again that although, as I had blithely assured the nurse, I did speak the language, England was to me a foreign country. I had visited once or twice for conferences, attended by OM teams from all over the world, but I had never met many English people or gone out to visit other places. I hadn't even met Ron's relations yet, and the money system was still a complete mystery. It seemed I had a lot to learn.

Over that weekend I settled down in the hospital that was to be my home—for how long? 'Rehabilitation' sounded like rather a long-term activity. I had little chance to brood, however, for every minute of the day seemed to be filled. First I was visited by a doctor with my old friends, the pins and little steel hammers to test sensation and reflexes. Then there were temperatures, tea, bed-pans, tea, meals, more tea—something was always happening.

In between all this I began to get to know the other inhabitants of the ward. As I lay there in the long room, I listened alertly to the chatter that filled it, fitting names to voices, for it was impossible to see my companions' faces from my horizontal position.

Dolores was from Lewisham, and she was the most vociferous and friendly of guides to this new world. She was bedfast herself, but she introduced me by name to each of the women, giving me details of their lives and their medical conditions which would have done credit to a student doctor. She herself had had a spinal operation and was in Stanmore for four months for after-care.

Most common on the ward were older women having hip operations, and those who had discs removed from the spine. These latter were a great encouragement: they were admitted almost immobile, their bodies racked with pain, and after three weeks they left, able to touch their toes and feeling marvellous. The wonders of such medicine revived my flagging spirits as I watched each departure.

I was moved to a position in the middle of the ward, and Barbara, in the next bed, became a close friend of mine. We talked for hours together. Her husband was a doctor, and they had been living in Rhodesia with their four children when she was diagnosed as having polio. She was flown to England for medical care, leaving her family behind, and now she was completely paralysed down to her waist, though her feet and legs remained unharmed.

As I got to know people, my mind was increasingly filled with their various dilemmas, and I made an effort to pray for them one by one. Imagine Barbara, an active wife and mother, suddenly stricken helpless. The whole issue of why people suffer began to raise questions I had never asked before. 'Lord, what hope can I offer Barbara?' I questioned. In the intervals of hospital life, I found I had plenty to think about.

I missed Ron, of course, but the other women on the ward were very friendly, and although I knew no one in England and so had no visitors, I looked forward to visiting time and the influx of new faces and voices. Many of the other patients were there for fairly long stays, so I got to know their families and friends and chatted to them too.

Ron went back to work for OM, and was busy preparing for the 1965 conference which was to be held in Birmingham, so he was travelling all over the country. The hospital staff were immensely helpful to us, and allowed him to visit at odd hours of the day and night whenever he was passing through London. On several occasions they even gave him breakfast when he called in on his way to catch an early train, though he had to run the gauntlet of much ribald comment from the other women on the ward.

"'Ere, 'owe did you get in so early?' Dolores would inquire. 'I think 'e's spent the night under the bed, girls!'

Poor Ron was so shy, he would arrive at my bedside crimson with embarrassment.

I loved to hear of all he was doing, and was delighted that he was back at work, and able to do something other than nurse me. I felt guilty that my survival had taken all the efforts of both of us, and my independent spirit liked to think that at least he was able to go and live his life normally once more.

On Monday I waited impatiently for the ward rounds when I would meet the consultant and the specialists who would be dealing with my case. I was anxious to know what treatment I would be receiving, how long it would take, and what the prognosis was. I knew how far I'd come in three months, but I had no idea how much I would be able to achieve, or how long it would be before I could leave the hospital. I had a dim vision of spending endless months in physiotherapy, but I pushed it to the back of my mind and greeted the approaching flurry of white coats with a smile.

'Good morning, Mrs George,' began the consultant, and my heart sank. I was so used to the informality of the hospital at Belgrade—conditions there might have been chaotic, but my relationship with Dr Simic had been warm. Indeed, by the time we left, I felt like a daughter to him; he had confided his personal feelings to me, especially his search for meaning in life, and I in my turn had shared my fears and hopes with him—even more than I had with Ron. Now, it seemed, I was faced by the famous British reserve; it was clear that no such intimate relationship was to be expected with one's consultant here.

'I have looked at the X-rays,' the doctor went on, unaware of my reaction, 'and we really cannot quite decide what to do with you.'

He sat down beside my bed to explain, then got up again as he realised that he had disappeared from my view. Frowning slightly, he went on,

'The treatment you had in Belgrade was only partly successful: you understand that they were trying to allow the misplaced vertebra to slip back into alignment? Well, it has almost done so—almost, but not quite. It's still a little out of line, and it's pressing on a motor nerve. That means that as long as it does so,

72

you will be unable to regain full control of the left side of your body.'

I lay silent, unable to speak. When Dr Simic told me that the treatment had worked, he had indeed said that the vertebra was 'almost aligned', but I hadn't realised the implications. I'd thought that I needed only the rehabilitation treatment in England to restore me to full movement—but now the doctors above me were discussing between themselves whether a further operation was necessary. I decided it was time to remind them that I spoke English.

'What are the problems?' I asked. 'Why are you unsure about doing the operation?'

One of the other doctors looked at me in surprise as I broke into their conversation.

'Well,' he said, 'open-neck surgery is rather risky—there's always the possibility that we could cause more damage. And then it's been so long since the accident that your bones will have begun to fix themselves into these positions. It would be very difficult to initiate more movement.'

I winced at the thought. I really didn't want any more operations—I never wanted to see the inside of an operating theatre again. But I didn't think, somehow, that telling them that would have much effect on their decision. All I could do was wait and see what the verdict was.

Chapter 5

It was not until Thursday that the consultant and his entourage stopped by my bed again.

'Good morning, Mrs George,' he said. 'We have decided not to operate. We think that the possible improvement would be minimal, and not sufficient to outweigh the risks.'

'Well, thank goodness for that,' I smiled. 'I really wasn't very keen on being operated on again. What happens now?'

The consultant turned to the physiotherapist beside him.

'You will have your own individual plan worked out, giving you the physiotherapy you need. I have already explained that you are unlikely to regain full movement on your left side, but we will make sure that you utilise to the full all the movement that is available to you.'

'What does that mean, doctor?' I asked. 'Do you think I will be able to walk again? Or at least sit up in a wheelchair?' I was very aware that I was still horizontal, and even being raised to sit up still seemed an impossible task.

The consultant laid his bundle of notes on my bed,

and leaned over me so that I could see his face. His cool and distant manner left him for a moment as he spoke very earnestly.

'Mrs George, you must believe me when I say that how much you achieve is entirely up to you. In cases like yours, so much depends on your own attitude. If you are determined to get well then you can achieve almost anything. Most of your motor nerves are intact. Your left side may always be awkward and lazy, but you should be able to walk—if you work hard at it. How much progress you make, and how fast you make it, depends on your will to improve.'

Really, if I had been able, I would have jumped off the bed and flung my arms around his neck. At that moment my worst fears were left behind for ever: I need not be dependent on others to look after me. I wanted to yell with delight—but I spared some concern for his British reserve. He moved away from the bed with a smile, and on to his next patient, leaving me with a great deal to think about.

I felt that he had offered me a challenge, and I was determined to do my best. I had every motivation to succeed: I was young, newly married, with everything to live for. I decided right then that I was going to be the best patient they had ever had! Besides, the consultant didn't know that he was calling on the one thing I knew was within my powers. I might be weak and feeble and disabled, but I'd always been strong-willed. 'Stubborn', my mother called it, but now I knew that my great failing was about to become my greatest asset.

I threw myself wholeheartedly into the hospital routine. Most of it was the same as ever—I was still being turned every couple of hours, for instance—but there was something different about the quality of the care I was receiving. I was at least able to co-operate more when the nurses turned me, since I had regained some movement, and because the majority of the nursing staff were female, I felt more relaxed about the whole operation.

My hair was beginning to grow back, which gave me an enormous psychological boost, and I was astounded to find that a hairdresser came to cut, wash and style it! As my hair hadn't been washed at all in Yugoslavia, the difference was amazing. She also gave me a manicure. Suddenly I began to take an interest in my appearance. I began to feel like a woman again, and not just an inanimate lump of broken body.

When I first arrived in Stanmore, I wondered how I would ever bear living in a huge ward with all those other people, after the enclosed privacy of my room in Belgrade. Yet it was cheering to hear other voices, laughing or complaining about the agonising physio. There was no language barrier to make communication difficult, and we were all women together, with our shared viewpoint and similar concerns. I gained a lot of support from the other patients.

Then there was the lady from the WRVS who came and wrote letters for me, made the appointments for the hairdresser, and brought round the little library trolley and helped me to find new books to read. The whole sense of caring was utterly different from the hospitals in Yugoslavia. This may have been because most of the nurses were women, while in Yugoslavia they were men. At any rate, the psychological improvement was immense.

As I lay in my bed I often heard the other women complaining about the food, the nurses, or various little inconveniences of hospital life, but nothing could

77

detract from my growing appreciation of the NHS and the privilege of becoming part British by marriage.

Meanwhile the treatment went on apace. My physiotherapist discovered that my left shoulder was atrophying because of the extended period of immobility, so I had to have a general anaesthetic while it was manipulated, followed by twice-daily physiotherapy.

Every day we worked to increase the range of movement in my limbs and the strength of my lazy muscles, and gradually I began to see results. I no longer needed help to turn in bed, and the pressure sores were healing well. After a couple of weeks Julie, the physiotherapist, arrived by my bed as usual.

'Right, Nancy,' she said brightly. 'I think it's time you had a different view. This afternoon you can sit up and have a good look at the world. What do you think of that?' She never found out what I thought. I was speechless as she strode off down the ward, calling greetings to various patients as she went.

Sitting up! I was delighted, horrified, terrified and amazed all at once. I hadn't expected it to happen so soon, I had longed for it, and now I was desperately frightened, just as I had been when the traction was first removed. What if I fell off the bed? (I knew the nurses would never let that happen, but why let logic restrain you when you're having a really good worry?)

That afternoon the two nurses laughed at the expression on my face as they approached the bed.

'Come on, Nancy, don't look so scared,' they said. 'We aren't going to drop you, you know.'

Very slowly the bed was tilted up until I was almost in a sitting position, with a nurse on either side to support me.

'Yo, ho, and up she rises,' carolled Dolores as I

gradually rose into view. And what a view. I felt dizzy with the new perspectives as the long room appeared, together with the faces of the other patients, whom I'd known only by their voices for so long. Dolores was the greatest surprise—I'd imagined her as a big, thickset woman, with a frame to match her powerful voice which dominated the ward, commenting on everything. I could hardly believe that she was the petite lady in the bed opposite mine.

'Nice to meet you, Nancy,' she said, grinning impishly. 'Gone a bit pale, haven't you, love?'

It was true. For a horrible moment I thought I was going to faint completely, as the room swam and a buzzing sounded in my ears.

'It's OK,' said one of the nurses comfortingly. 'Your heart isn't used to having to pump your blood uphill yet, so it's finding it rather a strain. You'll soon get used to it.'

In fact the bed had only been inclined at about twenty degrees, but I felt as if my head was miles up in the air. I was restored to a horizontal position after only a few minutes, and I would never have believed that I would be so glad to lie down again! But after that, I sat up for a little longer each day, and each day the angle of the bed was increased. The pressure sore on my bottom was continuing to heal, so that eventually I was able to sit up in what was almost a normal position. I was surprised at how uncomfortable it was to begin with. I had no tone at all in my stomach muscles, and the effort of holding my body upright left me feeling strained and sick—but again my body adapted in time.

I began to feel rather complacent; why, this was almost like normal life! Eating a meal sitting up was one of my greatest satisfactions, and reading was much easier, too. Conversation with other patients was much more fun when I could see them. I conveniently forgot that I was still totally confined to bed: I had enough new experiences and hard work to keep me occupied.

Nevertheless, the physiotherapists didn't intend to waste any time.

'Is Ron coming in to see you over Christmas?' inquired Julie one day, after a particularly strenuous session.

'No, I'm afraid not,' I replied. 'He has to be away. He always manages to ring me, though.'

'Never mind, I've got a present for you,' she answered. 'How would you like to eat your Christmas dinner out of bed, sitting on a chair?'

First I was wheeled to the plaster room, where my head, neck and shoulders were encased in plaster of Paris, and once this was dry it was cut away and used as a model for a styrofoam brace. This turned out to be a flesh-coloured plastic cocoon which supported my head and neck while I was sitting up. I quickly got used to wearing it whenever I was to be moved anywhere, and as it also concealed the bald places on the back of my head, I was quite grateful for it when meeting visitors.

On Christmas Day I awoke with the familiar sense of mixed excitement and dread that accompanied every new step. What if I fell out of the chair? I was sure I wouldn't be able to balance! Up the ward marched the sister, carrying a large armchair, and followed by three nurses. The curtains around my bed were drawn and the bed tilted up to the sitting position. Then the nurses lifted me out onto the chair.

It was the most unpleasant Christmas present I ever hope to have. I sat for ten minutes in that chair, rigid with fear of falling sideways, racked with nausea and dizziness, seeing nothing but the bed curtains enclosing me. When they put me back to bed, I fell at once into an exhausted sleep, and almost missed the promised Christmas dinner entirely!

When Ron made his regular telephone calls he was delighted with the progress I was making. So was I, really, though often I was simply too tired to sound suitably enthusiastic. I was sorry he wasn't with me to share everything, but I was grateful that he had returned to normal life, unrestricted by my problems. The most important thing was that he was back at work—not just because it was a more normal life for him than nursing me in hospital, but because he was pressing on with the work of mission to which we were both called. Even through the worst times of my illness, when I felt weakest and most wretched, I had never lost the deep assurance that God's plan for us was that we should work together for his kingdom, bringing people to know Jesus Christ. For that reason I never resented Ron's absence when I was in hospital: for one thing, there were always people around me to whom I could talk and for whom I could pray; and for another, it felt right that he should be continuing our work outside the hospital so that I could eventually join him.

I knew that Ron and others were praying for my healing, and certainly my daily improvement witnessed to God's faithfulness in hearing those prayers. Yet there was no blinding flash, no instantaneous miracle: it was all hard slog, each new stage in recovery accomplished with pain and effort and the loving help of nurses and doctors. But it seemed to me no less miraculous for that.

After the initial shock of sitting up in a chair on Christmas Day I tried harder to get back to normal positions and normal movements: on Boxing Day I sat in a chair for an hour. Just facing life in a perpendicular position set my mind racing: my dreams of normal living were beginning to come true. As I squirmed uncomfortably, trying to avoid that bedsore cavity on my bottom, I found myself using my left side more. I asked if I could get dressed each day, and the ward sister rang Ron to ask him to bring in loose trousers, a blouse and a matching sweater for me, with some underwear. This was a new struggle: even with help, I found dressing myself took so long, and was so exhausting, that I would gladly have gone back to bed afterwards, if only it hadn't meant taking everything off again!

A few days after Christmas, as I was sitting in the armchair by my bed (somewhat more comfortably by then), two nurses came and stood one on each side of me.

'Time to stand up!' they said brightly, and before I could protest they took an arm each and hefted me to my feet. Thus propped up, vertical for the first time since September, I blinked in amazement. My legs were shaking beneath me and I looked down in wonder to see that I really was standing on my own two feet. I was horrified by the sight of my legs—the muscles had wasted away, and I had become very thin. They looked spindly and pathetic, hardly strong enough to support me. But they did, and there I was—helped, supported, but undeniably standing.

I smiled at the nurses through a haze of tears. I had done it. Up until then I had hardly dared to believe that I really could walk again, but once on my feet I simply knew that I would manage to move. It was like a promise from God, a token of what he would accomplish in me. My wavering faith, my moments of despondency, my times of weary self-pity that every simple task should be such an effort, all slid away from me like the pilgrim's burden which rolled off down the hill at the foot of the cross. As I sank back thankfully into my chair, my heart was full of praise.

Once again there was no time to reflect on my achievement. The very next day Fred, our bouncy orderly, rolled a wheelchair up to my bed.

'We've got a date to go out, me darlin. You're going to the gymnasium for an hour and I get to take you,' he said. He loaded me into the wheelchair, helped me to fit on the brace to support and protect my neck, and pushed me out of the ward, whistling as he went.

I always enjoyed being taken out of the ward, through the covered walkways in the open air, and to another part of the hospital. Even in the coldest weather it was pleasant to breathe the fresh air, and have a new view. It was particularly exciting now that I was sitting up in a chair, and could see so much more—even though the old army barracks which made up most of the Stanmore Hospital were not very beautiful. The sky was a brilliant blue, the sun shone brightly, and the cold, crisp wind was most welcome to my distorted sensations. I felt I had begun to live again.

The gym had another charm: it was used by out-patients. This meant that real people, wearing real clothes came there! It was strange, somehow—I'd become so used to seeing everyone in nighties, or nursing uniforms, apart from the occasional visitor. It was like being allowed a glimpse of the outside world, the world I would one day rejoin.

I was greeted by Julie, the physio who had worked

83

so hard with me on the ward, pushing and pulling to my syncopated groans. She stood in the middle of a startling array of mats, steel bars, wooden steps and all sorts of strange contraptions. My corner of the gym seemed to be entirely surrounded with mirrors.

'What are those for?' I asked, curiously.

'Oh, they're to encourage you,' replied Julie. 'Once you see yourself standing and walking you'll believe you can do it! And you can correct your posture more easily if you can see yourself.'

That was when I realised what would fill my next hour in the gym. Fred stayed long enough to get me out of the wheelchair and into an ordinary straight wooden chair facing a set of walking bars.

'Don't leave me now, Freddie,' I begged. I trusted his strong arms.

'Off you go,' retorted Julie. 'We'll see you in an hour.'

She talked to me for a while, explaining just how she planned to get me on my feet between two bars in front of all those telling mirrors. Then she called a second physio to help her support me.

'If you just stand up once today for a few seconds between the bars,' she said, 'you'll have made all those weeks of work worthwhile.'

'I've only done it once, you know,' I reminded her nervously, 'and that was only for a moment. It made me feel awfully strange.'

'Up you come,' said Julie, quite unmoved by my protests. I gave an arm to each of the girls.

'OK, let's go,' I said.

I made several determined but unsuccessful attempts. Julie repositioned my feet, she and Karen changed arms to support my back, and with the next push I was up. I just glared at my feet, wondering how long I could last.

'Straighten up,' giggled Julie, 'and look at yourself in the mirror. You'll be all right.'

I wasn't. As I lifted my head and tried to focus my eyes, suddenly the floor seemed to move—first sideways and then up and down. The room swam, the mirrors swayed around me nauseously. I straightened myself to stand upright, and the whole world danced dizzily around me.

'I think I'd better sit down,' I gasped.

They helped me to sit, and Karen rushed for a plastic bowl—just in time.

'Well done, Nancy,' I heard Julie saying over and over again, as I vomited into the bowl.

'Sure, well done indeed,' I thought. I felt miserably sick and embarrassed. Slowly the gym came back into focus and the floor stopped heaving.

'Is it always like that?' I asked.

'Oh, don't worry, it often happens the first time,' said Julie. 'Your body's having to make too many adjustments at once. Now that your tummy's empty, you're not likely to be sick again. Want to try it once more?'

I couldn't bear the thought of defeat so I agreed to try it again. This time I watched my feeble image in the mirror instead of my feet as I rose from the chair. I did it more quickly and felt less dizzy. The girls placed my hands on the bars and moved away, leaving me to stand alone for a brief minute—well, sixty-four seconds to be precise.

'You did it!' exclaimed Julie. 'You stood on your own for more than a minute! Aren't you thrilled?'

I had to admit that I'd dreamed of triumph in the gym: I'd imagined myself walking that first day. It wasn't exactly the success I'd hoped for. Besides, my legs felt like blancmange, and my right hand was marked by my own nails where I'd gripped the bar so hard. My stomach still felt nauseated and my head was light. I could hardly describe the experience as thrilling.

Now the gym was added to my routine, and I looked forward to my daily stints. I had to retrain my mind to move my muscles, consciously willing each movement. Soon I took my first steps between the two bars, sliding the lazy left foot in front of the right. Julie's humour and hard-driving workouts made me determined to walk. She didn't allow me to slide that left leg for many lengths of the bar. I had to concentrate, learning to think through each step: bend the left knee, pick up the foot, set it down gently.

I watched my movements in the mirrors (mercifully the nausea never returned after that first day) and tried to persuade my unwilling left side to do as well as the right. It didn't look very graceful, but I was getting along unaided. That fact alone kept me going when I was tired out, and encouraged me to drive my weak muscles on to greater efforts. There was something else, too. In the first week of January Ron would be back and able to visit me, and I wanted to walk to him. I returned to the ward each day exhausted and exhilarated.

The other physiotherapy continued alongside my walking practice. I exercised with weights in my hands to develop strength in the muscles, and watched with delight as my arms began to fill out again.

In the rehabilitation centre I tried basket-weaving, which was used to improve the concentration, as well as the fine movement in the fingers. Somehow that basket-weaving irritated me. I knew what its purpose was, but it seemed so irrelevant. Fine as a hobby, a craft skill, or even just as exercise, but I couldn't persevere with it. It seemed pointless: I didn't want to make baskets. It worked, though, and I could see the improvement in my right hand, though the left refused to perform very well. Again I was hampered by the fact that the left hand could feel things, but not manoeuvre properly, while the right was much more flexible but unable to sense anything.

One day I looked down at my hands in exasperation, remembering all the things I used to do with them unthinkingly. Dressing myself, writing letters, brushing my hair, icing a cake, playing the piano, typing... That was it! Typing.

Maybe basket-weaving wouldn't help me to regain my independence, but typing could! That day I arrived in the rehabilitation centre full of a new idea.

'Please, instead of the basket-weaving, couldn't I do some typing? I'm sure it would have the same effect on my fingers, and I'd be much better at it!'

The good-humoured physio in charge of the department looked thoughtful.

'Well, we've never been asked that before, but I suppose you're right. OK, I'll see what we can do.'

The next morning a manual typewriter was waiting for me, and I began work enthusiastically, relearning to type with one hand. I attacked the task with my usual vigour, and made the fingertips of my right hand quite sore with practising! I knew that I was not only improving my dexterity, but working at something useful, and it helped me enormously. It was good to feel that I was engaging in a real activity, something that would help me to make my way in the world.

The next event was swimming in the hydrotherapy pool twice weekly, taking the place of workouts in the gym. I enjoyed that immensely, since I mixed with outpatients who came in just for swimming. Conversations expanded beyond the hospital walls as I talked to ordinary people living in a real world—a world of current events, television programmes, children, shopping. I appreciated the stimulus of meeting new people, and became aware of all sorts of English-American differences. It was a high spot in my week.

As I increased in strength and confidence so my co-ordination in walking increased. The stretched-rubber-band feeling in my stomach was declining and I found myself chancing a few steps barely holding on to the bars. After a couple of weeks Julie gave me a walking-frame to take back to the ward so that I could walk about alone. My first solo walk to the bathroom was another major step towards that coveted independence!

I was very aware that the God who had guided the surgeon's hands in Yugoslavia still had his hand firmly on every stage of my progress. Yes, I had to work, I had to co-operate with the medical staff overseeing my care—but ultimately it was God who was giving me back my faculties. It made me feel honoured that he loved me that much.

In a way, my spiritual life reflected my physical life. After that cataclysmic event, my body was broken and my responses confused, yet I was still alive, and my life went on. Similarly, my prayer life and Bible reading were totally disrupted, my emotions were muddled, and many times, like Job, I asked, 'Why me?'

Yet underneath, my faith in a loving Father was alive, and continued to sustain me.

I knew that for a long while I'd been carried by the prayers of many people other than myself. My own prayers were introspective, and I missed the vibrant companionship I'd become accustomed to in team life. I wanted to get to know God better, and I began to use my free time to read books written by Christians older than myself. I tried to read the Bible with enthusiasm because I felt that I should, yet I understood little. It was hard to concentrate.

My mind was in a turmoil. I felt that I needed a vision like Job's, something that could make sense of the suffering of others, and the pain which I still endured, in spite of the bright hopes and exciting progress. I knew God's love for his world—love so great that Jesus came to share our pain and show the way. How did all these things fit together? Why couldn't I see the whole?

I was full of gratitude to God for my healing, but I was very aware of the many who suffered from illness, accident or anxiety, without any apparent improvement. I was particularly close to Barbara, and I knew of her fears for the future. How could she ever take care of her young family, disabled as she was? I shared with her many of my fears, my hopes and my faith in the Father God who cares for all his children.

I was struck by how easy it was to talk to other patients about such things. It was as though our common experiences of suffering, pain and despair gave us a link, enabling us to cut through the usual bright superficial chat. Even once I was able to walk around the ward with a stick, it was clear to anyone that I was not 'whole', not normal and unscathed. A limp was like a badge declaring our shared experience.

One day at visiting time I was chatting to an elderly gentleman, who asked me when my accident happened.

'September,' I replied.

He smiled at me sadly. 'My daughter died in September,' he said, 'several years ago, it was.'

I began to say how sorry I was, but he went on.

'I always think about her specially in the autumn. It seems a suitable time for things to die. It looks like the end of things, doesn't it? But you know, it's only because the leaves fall that the tree is able to take the weight of the winter snow. And in time there's new growth, and new life. No, I don't believe it is the end.'

That evening, when visiting time was over, and the ward was quiet once more, I settled down to sleep, but the old man's words kept running through my mind. The image of the fallen leaves seemed so close to my own experiences.

I thought of autumn walks I had enjoyed in the past—the golden sunlight, the brisk wind, the crunch of dead leaves underfoot. I remembered how as a child I would throw armfuls of raked-up leaves in the air and watch them fall twirling all around me, and smell the earthy, invigorating smell of the damp leaf-mould.

Yet individually, each dead leaf wasn't beautiful: its shape was distorted as it dried and crumpled, the veins protruded, the colour died from green and gold to dirty brown. It was dead and spoiled, and no one cared that it existed. That was how I'd felt—mis-shapen and useless.

Yet autumn is only a part of the great cycle of the year. One by one the leaves die and fall to the ground, and the stripped trees stand naked in the winter sunlight. Who could imagine, then, the beauty of the new life to come in spring?

I rolled over in bed and snapped on the dim night-light. My Bible was lying on the table beside me, and that day's reading had been from Philippians. 'Christ will transform our lowly bodies so that they will be like his glorious body' (Phil 3:21). It was a promise which seemed the dearer to me now that every action of my body was achieved with such effort.

Was it a careless act of fate that I had broken my neck at the start of my career, the start of my life? It was an event like the fall of a dead leaf, ugly and debilitating. Yet it must be part of a greater plan, just as one leaf is part of the life of the tree, the forest, the world.

As I turned off the light and drifted into sleep, I thought of the beauty of the heaped golden mounds of dead leaves, every one a suffering and a sacrifice, ready to be used for the next year's growth.

Chapter 6

I was sitting up, with Ron perched on the bed beside me, his arm around me tightly. Our little plot had worked perfectly.

One nurse was posted as lookout, and she spotted him approaching along the corridor. At her signal, two other nurses helped me to my feet and propped me up with my sticks for support. I'd planned to walk to meet my husband, but somehow when I saw him framed in the doorway all the strength seemed to drain out of my legs, and I just stood and waited for him to come to me. He hurried up the ward and took me in his arms, holding me as if I might break in his hands, and then kissed me, oblivious to the cheer that went up from the other beds!

We closed the curtains round the bed to give us some privacy, we prayed together, and now Ron was excitedly telling me of what he had been doing, and beginning to make plans.

At home he was staggering under the weight of correspondence. That year, 1965, was the year of the great OM conference, which was being held in Birmingham, and friends from all over the world would be in England for a week. Many of them had been praying for us ever since the accident, and Ron had been passing on news of my recovery at every stage. He was involved in the general organisation for 200 people, and dozens of them had written asking whether they might come and visit me.

'At this rate, we'll have to hire coaches to bring them all down here from the conference centre,' he grinned happily. 'Do you think you'll be well enough to cope with some visitors?'

It was a chance too good to miss—so many old friends together at one time.

'Sure I will, honey,' I replied. 'But I'm not sure if the hospital can cope. I guess we'd better ask the Sister if it's OK.'

Ron was slightly nervous of Sister Drew, the forceful and determined nurse who had effected my removal from the airport so efficiently only a month ago. Nevertheless he went off to find her, and explained his errand. She came back with him to my bed.

'I'm sorry, Nancy. I realise that you've had hardly any visitors since you've been with us. But making up for it all in one weekend isn't really possible. No one would be able to move in here.'

I was disappointed, but also mystified by the twinkle in her eye. She was smiling at Ron.

'I've a better idea. What if Nancy were to go to them? I'm quite willing to let her go home for a weekend, if someone is willing to take responsibility for her. Would you do that?'

Would he! We could hardly believe our luck. I almost thought Ron was going to hug her as well!

'Do you really think Nancy will be well enough to spend a whole weekend out of the hospital?' he asked.

94

Sister Drew looked at me. 'What do you think, Nancy?'

I grinned at her. 'I'll give it my best shot,' I replied.

'I thought you might say that,' she said. 'Now, this conference is in ten days' time, is that right? Well, I think we'd better have a dry run. Today's Thursday. Get a good night's sleep tonight, and you can go home with Ron tomorrow for the weekend. Then if you come back all in one piece, we'll have an idea of how you'll cope with a hundred visitors next weekend. OK?'

'I'll say!' I responded enthusiastically. I couldn't believe it. An hour earlier I'd had no thought of leaving the hospital for months to come. Now, suddenly, I was going home that very weekend.

The next day Julie helped me to practise getting in and out of a car, by stepping up a low step and sliding on to a chair. I wasn't taking any medication—not even sleeping tablets—so there was no need to take anything with me except my walking sticks. Ron arrived and signed a daunting-looking document, saying that he took full responsibility for my well-being, and we stepped outside into the fresh air. It was my first taste of freedom, my return to the real world, but the moment was quite lost on me. I stood still in amazement, staring at the vehicle waiting by the door. It was yet another VW van, not unlike the one we'd abandoned in Yugoslavia, complete with a sliding door and a step that looked to me only slightly more accessible than Mount Everest.

'I'll never get into that,' I gasped. 'I've been practising for a car!'

Somehow they got me into the passenger seat, and Sister Drew slammed the door.

'Be careful,' she called as Ron started the engine. I

couldn't turn my head because of the styrofoam brace, but I knew that the other nurses had gathered at the door to see me off. So I did a regal wave from the window and we drove away from Stanmore Hospital for the first time.

Curiously, I wasn't in the least afraid of driving again. Nothing about the journey reminded me of the last time I'd been in a van, when the accident had happened, and I simply looked about me in delight, at the lighted shop windows and the busy London streets.

We were on our way to Fulham, in south-west London, where an OM team member owned a small grocery shop with rooms above it. We probably couldn't have found a less suitable place if we'd searched for a week. For a start, the living accommodation was up two flights of stairs. We hadn't thought about practising stairs. Ron walked beside me, one friend pushed from behind and another pulled from above, and somehow they got me up. I was ready for a rest, but Joan and Peter Barrie, with whom Ron had been living, always had a prayer meeting in the flat on Friday evenings. So I arrived, tired and dishevelled, at the top of the seemingly endless stairs, to find a room full of people. They all knew my story, of course, and one man kept exclaiming, 'You're just like Lazarus, my dear, just like Lazarus.'

I remember very little of that evening. After the peace and quiet of the hospital, just being in the tiny room full of people was confusing. I was struck by the colour and warmth of my surroundings, the patterned curtains and the thick carpets, after the clinical white of the ward. I felt as though I had been starved of stimulus for months, and my weary brain simply couldn't take it all in. Someone thrust a cup of tea in my hands, and I drank it thirstily. I half wished I could hide away—I felt less like Lazarus than something from outer space, sitting there in my pink plastic headgear. I hated being the centre of attention, and though I joined in the prayers of thanksgiving with heartfelt warmth, I longed for privacy.

At last it was over. The bedrooms, of course, were on the top floor—up yet another flight of stairs—but Joan and Peter had thoughtfully allowed us to use their room, which had a double bed, while they squashed into Ron's room. Exhausted by the journey, the excitement, the company, and the stairs, I undressed slowly and sank into bed thankfully. It was the first time Ron and I had been alone together, sharing a bed, in a private room at home, for four months.

I found I wasn't quite as tired as I had thought.

I had to be back in the hospital on Monday morning in time for my session of physiotherapy. I raced back, like Cinderella, dutifully did the session in the gym, then went to bed and slept for two days. In the middle of the week I ran a temperature, and I was in an agony of nerves lest the doctors refused to let me out again. However, they gave their assent. It wasn't until much later that I learned how unusual it was for a patient at my stage of recovery to be allowed home at weekends; fortunately I seemed to benefit so much that they adopted it as a general policy. Every trip out made me more aware of my disability, and more determined to overcome it. Each time I noticed some little thing—opening a tin or a jar, finding change in my purse—that I found difficult, but which I knew I could manage without help if only I worked that little bit harder at my physio exercises. The doctors were prepared to give me as much rope as I would take, and I was always prepared to take more than I could manage.

I spent Thursday and Friday mentally preparing myself for the weekend. I knew it would be hard work, meeting so many people, talking and smiling, but I was determined to do it. When Saturday morning arrived I was dressed and ready when Ron arrived, again in the battered old van. A nurse loaded a collapsible wheelchair into the back (which I was much too proud to use; it stayed there all weekend) and gave me my walking sticks. We were off.

'How many people are coming down to London, Ron?' I asked, as we drove away.

'None,' he replied. 'We aren't going to the flat in Fulham. We're going to Birmingham!'

I could hardly believe my ears. 'Ron, I'm sure that wasn't what Sister Drew meant when she said I could go home for the weekend.'

'That's OK,' he said. 'I just didn't say whose home you were going to!'

The long journey presented some difficulties: at that stage I was barely continent, and Ron quickly realised that when I said I had to go to the bathroom I meant NOW! Somehow we managed, and the friends who put us up in Birmingham were understanding and hospitable. I found I was thoroughly enjoying myself. While Ron attended the conference, I spent time with friends in a small room at the conference centre which had been set aside for me. I refused to use the wheelchair, but walked—very slowly—with my sticks, and sat in an ordinary chair in the little room while friends called in to see me.

Ron was so proud to have me there at his side, he was like a child with a new toy. He wanted me to speak at one of the meetings, but I really couldn't face that. However, I did attend one session when he told our story, and at his invitation I stood up where I was in the auditorium, while the assembled OM members clapped and cheered.

I went back that Sunday full of new hope and encouragement, not just from the applause and prayers of our friends, but from the sense of achievement I'd found. I had met dozens of people, and chatted and socialised as I had in the old days. Although I had never been alone in my little room— there was always a friend with me to help—I'd managed meals, and going to the toilet unaided. I didn't feel so dependent on Ron as I had expected. My real joy was going to church on Sunday and sitting in an ordinary congregation—I'd even worn a dress for the first time, though putting on tights with my one good hand was an exercise I didn't feel like repeating for a while!

It wasn't all success, though. I felt the strain of being constantly under observation, like a sort of showpiece. I wanted to give the honour to God, and acknowledge that my healing was under his hand, but I forgot that I was still the same old imperfect, human Nan that I'd always been. The result was that I smiled sweetly on the surface, and bottled up my tiredness and frustrations, so that once Ron and I were alone, my temper would suddenly flash out at him. Once when I almost fell getting out of the van, I let fly at him as if it was his fault. Why had he brought such an unsuitable vehicle? He expected too much of me too soon: why couldn't he learn to be a gentleman and help without being asked? Our evening was spoiled and we drove home in stony silence. I was ashamed of these outbursts, but couldn't seem to control them. I suppose it was all part of my mental adjustment to getting back in the world and taking responsibility for myself, but it reminded me sharply how easy it was to become a sour and spiky invalid.

From then on I was allowed out every weekend, and I progressed rapidly. To begin with we stayed in the inaccessible flat in Fulham, but later we went to Ron's aunt in Chelsfield. Ron liked us to go to St John's Church in Bromley, where the vicar was a close friend. I found this difficult as I was unfamiliar with the Anglican order of service, and I couldn't bob up and down during the prayers. I felt conspicuous in the neck brace I still had to wear, but I understood Ron's desire to show me off, and to demonstrate to people the answers to their intercession on my behalf.

The outings made my time in hospital much more endurable, too. Instead of the weeks stretching out endlessly before me, I now knew that I was in hospital for only a few days at a time, and the weekend breaks made the weekdays more purposeful.

The only problem seemed to be that I was still running this freak fever, which had the medical staff mystified. Then one day Sister Drew had an idea.

'Nancy,' she began, 'when you go home for the weekend, are you being careful?'

'Well, I try not to get too tired,' I replied, 'and I wear the neck brace when I'm walking and in the car...'

'That's not what I meant,' she said. 'Are you using a contraceptive?'

'Well, no,' I admitted. 'We sort of didn't bother...'

She roared with laughter. 'We'll run a pregnancy test, my girl, but I think we've found the reason for this temperature rise. And from the very first week-end, too!' And she went off down the ward, shoulders still shaking with laughter.

The test was positive, and Ron was thrilled. We couldn't think why it hadn't occurred to us, except that even walking had seemed so unlikely, the possibility of pregnancy seemed even more remote. The nursing staff obligingly kept quiet about it on the ward, but there was little chance of keeping our secret for long. I had no muscle tone at all after the months of lying in bed, and so the bulge began to show almost at once. My fellow patients noticed that I was putting on weight, and suggested that I wasn't as enthusiastic about my exercises as I might be. They were right—sitting and bending were still uncomfortable, and quickly became more so. When we told them the reason, they teased Ron unmercifully.

'I should watch 'er,' called out Dolores. 'You know our Fred, the orderly? Well, I know for a fact she goes out wiv 'im three times a week. They say they go to the gym, but I'm not so sure, now!'

Immediately the whole ward started on a knitting craze, and dozens of little bootees materialised seemingly overnight for the six-week bump that scarcely seemed like a real baby yet.

My own feelings were mixed. The doctors were planning to discharge me some time in April, and the baby was due in October. Like any young wife I had longed for a baby, but how would I manage a child, with the erratic lifestyle we had always lived, complicated by my disability and my poor balance?

Ron wasn't in the least worried by any of my fears. For him it was the fulfilling of his expectation—he'd been sure all along that I would be able to have his children—and he looked forward to October eagerly.

We began, for the first time since the accident, to discuss concrete plans for our future, once I was discharged from hospital. Our accommodation arrangements had already been made: I was going to live in the OM headquarters in Bolton, where I would have help available, so that Ron could be released from looking after me to carry on with his work.

However, there were longer-term plans to make. Before the accident we had intended to have a short holiday in England and the US, so that we could visit each other's families, and then go out to work for OM in India. It was a long-held dream for both of us that we should work for God in an Eastern country, and India held a special attraction. Was there any chance that we could still do it?

In addition, there was the question of further training. Ron had quit his training as a civil engineer one year before qualifying: disillusioned with the career prospects open to him, he had joined OM to take on a job he felt had more significance. My idea was that he should complete his training, either in Britain, the US or in France; he shared my feelings of unfinished business, but was equally willing to go to Bible College: he just wanted more discipleship, and didn't mind how he got it.

At this point George Verwer, who knew us both very well, had a private conversation with Ron.

'I still think you should consider India as your next posting,' he said. 'I've prayed about it for a long time and I still feel that you and Nancy are the people we need. You've both had plenty of experience of living in a foreign culture, and you have the right gifts for the tasks in hand there. Drena can help Nan with the baby, and there'll be the whole girls' team to help look after Nan. You needn't worry—she'll be in good hands.'

I have to admit I was pretty mad at George for suggesting it—I knew I was going to have trouble adapting to Bolton, let alone Bombay.

'And what about the training?' I protested. 'I thought we'd agreed that you were going to get properly qualified this time?'

'Yes, I know,' Ron agreed peaceably. 'But you know I don't really want a career in engineering. I'd be much happier doing the Bible College course. And George will be going to India with us: he's offered to direct my studies, as he'll be travelling and living with us.'

'Very kind of him, I'm sure,' I muttered ungratefully. Ron could see that I wasn't just upset about the move to India; it was all the uncertainty about how I would get through the next few months. Wisely he let the matter rest, and we prepared for my discharge first.

I had daydreamed intermittently about my departure from hospital, ever since I'd first got up on my feet. Illogically, I had seen myself completely able and whole, walking and moving exactly as I had before the accident, waving an emotional farewell to the hospital staff who had nursed me back to health. Needless to say, it wasn't quite like that.

I did hobble slowly down the ward saying goodbye to all my friends. I was touched by the affection and friendship I'd found there, but my feelings about leaving were quite overshadowed by my preoccupation with my pregnancy. I didn't feel I had much time or energy to spend on looking back: my body was calling to me urgently to look forward.

Neither was I able and whole. My co-ordination was quite good, and on my right side I had almost normal movement, but no feeling at all. I couldn't feel whether a cup of coffee was hot when I picked it up, or if I accidently touched the blade of a sharp knife. I had to watch what I was doing very carefully. My left side was very sensitive—I could feel the lightest touch, and even rough fabrics irritated me unbearably—but the movement there was very sluggish. I was learning to use my leg and arm, by swinging them round, but I could do very little with my hand.

Yet when I did look back I could only marvel at how far I had come. The damage at the time of the accident had seemed irrevocable, and yet I had achieved so much, with the help of so many people. How amazing that I had been put into the hands of Doctor Simic, probably the only doctor in Yugoslavia who had trained at Stoke Mandeville, the acknowledged centre of excellence in the treatment of spinal injury. How wonderful had been the care and concern of the staff at Stanmore. How unfailing had been the support of our friends, praying for us and writing to us. I felt as though God had prepared a chain of people, ready to aid and sustain me whenever I most needed their help. My healing wasn't instantaneous, and I knew that it was going to take more pain and effort yet, but I was assuredly being healed.

My new home in Bolton was in a pub which had been converted into a bookshop; there was living accommodation upstairs which was used by various OM team members, and I had a room on the first floor which I shared with Ron when he was there. I didn't need to cook, as communal meals were provided, but I learned to wash and iron clothes and generally to do the homemaking which had been postponed for so long. We had a bed and a desk, and Ron put up shelves for our books and built a raised changing area so that I wouldn't have to stoop to change nappies.

The bookshop was on a main street so I was able to go to the shops alone, though I couldn't carry much shopping, and the walk took me a long time. Twice a week an ambulance collected me and took me to the local hospital for a swim and a session of physiotherapy. My medical records had been transferred to Bolton, so they had a full picture of my condition when they began my ante-natal care.

In between preparing for the baby I was able to help downstairs in the office, which was good for my morale. I was accustomed to the office atmosphere and routine, and that, more than anything else, helped me to settle in to my new surroundings, especially when Ron was away so much.

There were many advantages to living in a community such as this: for one thing, I was never lonely, as there was always someone around to chat to. Physical help was always available for any task I was unable to manage—indeed, sometimes I had to dissuade people from doing everything for me!—and I knew that in an emergency there would always be someone within call. All this, together with the sympathetic support of a praying, caring Christian group made me feel very safe.

I didn't resent Ron's absence: the great thing was that he was the active part of our partnership. I knew that I was sustaining my share of the work by my prayers, by preparing for our baby and doing my best to get well. In time we would do God's work together again. Meanwhile, I took comfort from Paul's words: 'God has arranged the parts of the body, every one of them, just as he wanted them to be...the head cannot say to the feet, "I don't need you!" On the contrary, those parts of the body that seem to be weaker are indispensable' (1 Cor 12:21, 22).

Once I was properly settled in Bolton I had time to think and pray about our future, and almost at once I began to feel more at peace about the idea of going to India. I trusted George Verwer, and I knew he wouldn't have made the suggestion without a great deal of thought and prayer. He knew us both very well, had watched our relationship develop, and given us his blessing when we married. If he believed we could cope with the challenge of India, he was probably right! Besides, he and Drena had children of their own, so I knew I would have the benefit of all Drena's experience of motherhood—a reassuring thought! And we wouldn't be staying in the remote villages, but in the centre of Bombay, where European-style medical facilities would be available.

I wrote to my parents and took them into our confidence, asking for their guidance and advice. I didn't always agree with my mother, but she was someone whose opinion I trusted. My mother's reply was encouraging and positive.

'If God is in your plans,' she wrote, 'he will give you the strength and the ability to cope.' Then she went on, in a more motherly strain, 'How about Ron coming over to see us? We'd all like to get a look at your husband, you know, before you go off round the world again!'

Her words reminded me of the spirit in which Ron and I had set out on our married life, only a year before. We'd been willing then to take on the world in

God's name. I'd never wanted my disability to affect the life we'd agreed to share, and yet there I was, considering digging in my heels and asking to stay in Bolton! Suddenly all my fears began to seem ridiculous—the God who had cared for me and preserved my life from Yugoslavia to England could certainly be trusted to look after my family anywhere we went in his service.

When Ron joined me in Bolton after a month I told him of my changed feelings.

'But there's one thing I want you to do, first,' I added.

'What's that?'

'Well, you remember that originally we were going to visit the States so you could meet my family? Well, I still want you to do it.'

'But, Nan,' Ron protested, 'you can't possibly fly and travel all round the States now!'

'No, I know that,' I said. 'But you can. It's really important to me, Ron. I want my parents and my sisters and brothers to meet you before we set off again. I don't mind staying here while you go. Will you do it?'

Ron took a cheap flight to the US that summer, and visited my parents. He was rather apprehensive about it, but everything went well, and they were delighted to meet their son-in-law at last. He then took a ninety-day excursion ticket on a Greyhound bus, and travelled three thousand miles to the west coast, stopping en route to meet the whole family: Ruth, Bill, Betty, Lyle, Marian, Keith, Pat and Larry—and their husbands and wives and children! It was quite an undertaking for someone who came from a family of three, but Ron came through it all with flying colours, and a mental map of America studded with memories of homes and families where he was welcomed warmly.

At the end of his time there he spent another week with my parents, and shared with their home church the story of my accident and recovery, our progress and our plans. Many of the members of that church supported us in our work for OM, and their response was enthusiastic; they pledged to continue their support when we went to India.

Ron returned to Bolton very tired but happy; he found me well (and enormous). We settled down to work: I preparing for the baby, and he preparing to go to India.

When October arrived, the doctors informed me that they wanted me in hospital in plenty of time for the delivery, so that they could take every possible precaution; they also wanted me to spend eight days in hospital after the birth. They were surprised to learn that Ron wasn't at home: he was in London at a month-long conference. We had decided that he should have the maximum possible preparation for India, and that attending the conference would be more use to both of us than sitting at home waiting for my labour to start.

Drena came up to stay with me for a few days around the predicted delivery date, but the magic day came and went with no sign of activity. Drena was so anxious to be with me for the birth that we even went on a one-and-a-half-hour walk in an effort to get things moving, with no success. Ron was due to sail on 29th October, and I wanted to have the baby so that we could have lots of time together before he went; I knew I wouldn't be able to follow him for several weeks.

On 19th October Drena admitted defeat and went back to London; later that night I realised that I had at last gone into labour. I rang London to tell Ron the news, and the girl who answered the telephone had to fetch him from a prayer meeting.

'I'll come as soon as I can,' he said. 'Just hang on, Nan, till I get there!'

He slipped back into the prayer meeting and found George.

'Nan's gone into labour,' he murmured in his ear. 'I'm hitching up to Bolton now—I'll give you a ring tomorrow.'

'Fine,' said George. 'Give Nan my love.'

Ron had gone out of the room and was halfway down the stairs when George suddenly realised what he'd said. Leaping to his feet he sprinted after him and called down the stairs.

'Ron, you idiot, you can't hitch-hike! Take my car and drive! Here, catch!' and he threw his car keys down to him.

Back in Bolton I hung on as long as I could, and finally called the ambulance at 4 am.

'Aren't you the lady who was supposed to come in in plenty of time?' asked the nurse in the delivery suite.

'Well, yes,' I replied, 'but I just have to wait until my husband gets here!'

When he did arrive I was very pleased to see him, though I'm afraid it didn't show. The final stages of labour are not a time when a husband's calm cheerfulness is much appreciated. I was in agony, and Ron was trying to be positive.

'How about memorising a Psalm?' he suggested helpfully.

My reply, I regret, was rather rude.

In spite of this inauspicious start, he was allowed to stay for the birth, although in the end it had to be a forceps delivery—I just didn't have the strength to push the baby out.

They wrapped the baby and placed him in my arms, and Ron and I looked down at the tiny heart-shaped face of our son.

'Hello, Nathan,' I whispered. 'Isn't he beautiful, Ron?'

'He's lovely—from the front,' said my practical husband. 'Have you looked at him from the side? His head's completely flat!'

'That's just the delivery,' replied the nurse severely. 'He'll soon fill out and those forceps marks will fade. You should be grateful, you've got a perfect son and a very brave wife.'

Ron grinned up at her.

'Oh, I'm grateful, all right. Believe me, I am.'

Chapter 7

Nathan and I stayed in hospital for eight days and were discharged on 28th October, the day before Ron was to sail for India. We would fly out to join him after the six-week post-natal checkup.

Saying goodbye to Ron in the little room in Bolton was terrible. I felt utterly abandoned, weak and vulnerable, and the added responsibility of a tiny baby seemed too much. I was hit by a wave of depression which drowned even my delight in Nathan. However, I didn't want to convey any of this to Ron: I wanted him to go cheerfully, knowing that I was behind him, supporting him, and looking forward to following him. So I managed a smile as he waved goodbye.

I was glad that at least I wouldn't be entirely on my own: everyone in the HQ building was only too eager to help, and I had time to get used to handling the baby before my own journey. All the same, the two weeks while Ron was at sea were austere: I went through a deep valley of questioning, of wondering whether we were doing the right thing, of thinking we were both crazy—to go to a foreign country with a new baby and my handicap seemed like a mammoth task. During those weeks the Israeli-Arab war broke out, and the Suez Canal was closed: since I didn't know which side of it Ron was on, that added to my anxieties.

Nevertheless I recognised that weeping into the pillow wasn't going to help anyone—and I had a new baby to look after. I immersed myself in work, caring for Nathan, doing my exercises—I had post-natal ones as well as physiotherapy ones to do now!—and making preparations for joining the team in India. I had to apply for a passport for Nathan, and I sent off a copy of his passport photograph to Ron.

I prayed a great deal for a lightening of my mood, as I thought back over our decision to go to India: we trusted in the Lord to guide us, and if he was behind it, it couldn't be wrong, no matter how madcap it seemed!

We had no direct call to mission in India. Rather, we were aware of a great yearning for God which we both shared, an insatiable hunger to learn more about him and to direct our lives in his way. The odds had been against us in the early months of our marriage, but our experiences had deepened our longing to know that God is sovereign in suffering as well as in joy. We had disposed of most of our worldly goods: after the accident we lost all our wedding gifts and most of our luggage, and never found out where they ended up. It was a stripping down of even the few assets we had begun to build, forced upon us by circumstances, yet we didn't mind. We were determined to trust God for everything, and to see him work in our lives.

So our journey to India was contemplated initially because of our desire to be discipled, to be learners about God. Of course, we also wanted to discover another culture and learn from it; and we wanted to communicate to its people, and tell them something of our God, who is sufficient to meet every need.

George Verwer's offer to plan a learning programme for Ron was a timely one, coming just as we were realising this need for teaching. The idea was that Ron would study, write papers and work on projects, and also learn about a new culture under his guidance. George always worked at a frenetic pace, and encouraged others to do the same—you felt guilty if you didn't manage to achieve in each day as much as he did! At times I was dubious about Ron being tutored by this Gamaliel. Dearly though I loved both the Verwers, I didn't want our new marriage to be absorbed into their family life. I could imagine how George's infectious enthusiasm and powerful influence would challenge us, but I wanted it to be just that—a challenge. We would still have to make our own decisions about our lifestyle and methods of mission.

Meanwhile my spirits were lifted by Ron's letters, full of excitement about India and the new work.

'We docked in Bombay and got quite a reception,' he wrote. 'There seemed to be hundreds of coolies waiting for the ship, and there was chaos as they all ran to get jobs, carting the luggage and the cargo. Bombay is like an ant-hill; I don't know what the population is, but I've never seen anywhere so crowded. There's noise and movement all the time. Every day we go out with a tin trunk loaded with literature, and we have to identify the different nationalities in order to offer leaflets in the right languages: Gujurati, Hindi, Urdu, Tamil, and so on.

'The other night I was going to bed when I heard a scream from the office, and when I went to investigate, one of the girls was standing on top of our tin trunk, surrounded by rats. They gnaw through the wooden window frames to get to the food in the kitchen. I grabbed a broom and hit them on the head with it, and threw the bodies out of the window. They landed on the roof of a small building in the courtyard below, where the coolies sleep.

'It's impossible to keep the rats away: they are deemed to be holy here. The wealthy people who live in the other buildings overlooking this courtyard throw grain out of their windows to feed them. There are rat-catchers in the city, but they don't kill them: they trap them, take them outside the city and let them go.

'The poverty is terrible—not just among the beggars in the cities, but in parts of the countryside. You can travel through areas of great famine and need, like Bihar, and then go into the neighbouring state, Punjab, and see mounds of wheat stacked up by the roadside, waiting for the price to go up so the owners can make a bigger profit. Yet there are people dying of starvation in the next state, where the crops have failed. There's a great need for social action, to care for the poor and the sick, but I'm convinced that the primary need here is to preach the gospel, share the love of Christ and convert the human heart.'

How I longed to be with him, to share the sights, sounds and experiences of the new life he was already so involved in. The rest of the team who were currently in Bombay had passed through Belgrade while I was in hospital there, but I didn't know any of them well. One very close friend, Christa, an East German refugee, was at a Bible College in Madras, so I hoped to meet up with her at some stage, but otherwise I knew no one else. At first I thought about this mournfully, with a sense of isolation; then, as the weeks passed and more preparations were in train, with some interest; by the time two months had passed, I was feeling better, Nathan was clearly flourishing, and I was filled with excitement and a sense of adventure!

'Nan?'

Ron's voice sounded strange and distant on the crackly telephone line.

'Did you get my letter?'

'Yes,' I replied. 'I'm glad it's going well. How are you?'

'Fine... well, hot! How are you—and the baby?'

'We're doing great, just wait till you see us! Any news?'

'Yes, that's why I'm ringing. The money's through at last. You can book your flight as soon as you want. I'm looking forward to seeing you both. Missing you...'

The line went dead. So many things I wanted to say to him—still, I'd be able to say them in person soon.

I began some frantic telephoning round the airlines. The most direct flight was with Air India—great! A twenty-hour introduction to Indian culture—and perhaps I could practise my Hindi and Urdu on the stewardesses.

I travelled up to Chelsfield on a damp December morning and spent a weekend with Ron's Aunt Dolf and Uncle Tom, showing off Nathan and swapping baby-care hints with Mary, Ron's sister-in-law. On the Monday an old friend, Alf, arrived to take us to Heathrow. I was glad of Alf's cheerful friendliness that day: he carried the suitcases with ease, and explained our slightly eccentric luggage at the Air India desk with practised charm.

'Well, this suitcase is overweight because it's full of baby food...and this one is empty because the wheels of the carrycot will go in there when we take the pram apart...yes, this one's quite ordinary, just clothes...the carrycot's going as hand luggage, with the baby strapped on top...it's full because there are six tins of babymilk and a bag of disposable nappies underneath him.' Somehow he made it all sound quite sensible, really.

At last I waved him goodbye and was helped onto the plane and into my seat. We were off!

I had only flown twice in my life before: once when I was twelve, when I had to travel alone from Colorado to California to visit my sister—I hadn't enjoyed it at all, especially as the plane was diverted in bad weather and I was afraid I wouldn't be met at the airport. The other time was returning from Yugoslavia, when I was paralysed and strapped to a stretcher. In spite of these entertaining memories, I enjoyed the flight. The stewardesses spoiled us with lots of attention, and Nathan was contented, feeding and sleeping as though he were at home.

I had hoped to contact some friends in Beirut, but the head steward was unwilling to let me leave the plane without the baby and extra aid. So we used the two-hour wait constructively, and slept. Neither of us stirred until the aircraft taxied to take-off once more, and out came the bottle to keep Nathan sucking and happy.

I watched eagerly from the window as we approached Bombay, anxious for my first sight of our new home. On to the horizon came the grey miniature of a city, rapidly growing larger and expanding into detail: Bombay spreads along the coast, and the beauty of the blue ocean was breathtaking.

The plane taxied to a halt and the passengers hurried to leave, collecting baggage and carrying the coats they no longer needed. A stewardess helped me to assemble the carrycot on its wheels—as a pram it provided me with support while I walked back towards the terminal. I looked around: the building was thronged with people, a vast scurrying crowd. People were chattering incessantly, incomprehensibly; big burly men in white turbans, plump women in saris nursing a baby at the breast and minding another two or three toddlers: my first impression was of a sea of faces, all talking. I waited impatiently in the queue at the customs desk—somewhere out there would be a familiar face.

At last we were through, and a bagi watched the baby for me as I made my way through the crowd, searching anxiously—there! Ron was waving frantically, and we fought through the crowd and into each other's arms.

'Don't you want to see your baby?' I teased him after a moment or two, and he looked around for Nathan. I pointed out the pram, and he raced ahead of me to where Nathan lay on his back, stripped of everything but a nappy and a cotton top, smiling at the Indian bagi.

Ron stared at him. 'What on earth happened to that beautiful baby?' he asked. 'He looks as if you've pumped him up!'

'He's grown, silly. That photo I sent you was taken at nine days—you didn't expect him to stay the same!' It was true, the little heart-shaped face had grown chubby, but I resented any suggestion that he wasn't the most beautiful baby in the world.

As we waited for the luggage to arrive we sat in the van, trying to catch up the last two months apart. Ron told me about our accommodation, the food, the team—but it didn't seem necessary to take it all in at once. All we wanted was to be alone together, with our baby. It was only when we were on our way home that he mentioned casually what a good thing it was that we'd arrived on that particular day. We had the rest of the day together, and that night—but the very next day he had to leave with George for a three-week convention in Kerala! We were back to normal life.

We lived in the team house in Bombay with two other families, as Ron and George would be travelling together a good deal of the time. I knew that Drena would have prepared everything as well as possible for me, and I was glad to have her help in acclimatising to the new culture and to my new role as mother. One special gift that she had for us was a beautiful basket-weave cradle for Nathan, all lined in blue. I was delighted.

Nathan looked lovely in the pretty cot, but that first night I was up and down all night with him crying and fidgeting. I assumed that it was heat rash, and in the morning I consulted Drena.

'I'm worn out already,' I confessed. 'I had hoped he'd settle better than this. Do you think he'll get over this heat rash quickly?'

Drena took him and expertly slipped off his vest.

'That's not heat rash,' she said immediately. 'Those are bed-bug bites, look!'

Sure enough, Nathan's back and legs were covered with a trail of red bite-marks.

This was my first introduction to the bed-bug, and the beginning of a long war with the irritating little creatures. We'd seen them in Iran, but not often, and they hadn't really bothered us much. Here in India they seemed much more apparent, and Nathan's sensitive baby skin was particularly vulnerable.

On one memorable occasion Ron and I were waiting to meet a visitor at the railway station, and as the train was delayed we stopped for a meal at the station restaurant. Nathan was about fifteen months old, and able to walk, so we sat him on an ordinary chair. Quite soon he began to wriggle and fidget on the chair, and then to cry. We stood him up, and there, all across the back of his plump little legs, was a row of bites. Just then the waiter arrived with his notebook to take our order, seeing Ron holding the menu.

'Good day, Sahib,' he said. 'Would you like to order now? What can I get you?'

'TIC-20,' replied Ron tersely.

The waiter obviously thought he had misheard, and started scanning the menu for something which sounded similar, while I smothered my giggles in my handkerchief.

'TIC-20—bed-bug spray,' repeated Ron. 'Look at my son's legs. You have bed-bugs in your chairs!'

We never did get the bed-bug spray, and Nathan had his lunch sitting on my lap.

Our home was on the ninth floor of an apartment building. On the same floor was another flat which was used by the girls' team, and the office also functioned from there. This meant that Ron had only to cross the hallway to go to work, and the girls ate in our flat. The arrangement worked well, because all the children lived in one flat and weren't mixed with the office accommodation, and Drena and I had other company when the men were away travelling. It was

good to have the single girls in the team to relate to—
it stopped us talking baby talk all the time—and they
liked to take the children out sometimes, which gave
me the opportunity to rest.

My contribution to the community life was to do all
the shopping for forty people. Each week I would
gather together all the bags I could find and take
Nathan with me to the market. I went by taxi to a
large covered market in the centre of Bombay, and
there we soon became familiar figures. All Indians
seem to love children, so I was often able to leave
Nathan in the charge of a stallholder while I shopped
for rice, sugar, vegetables and other basic foods. The
only problem was that I had to take care to leave him
where the stallholder wouldn't feed him with unsuitable foods such as raw fruit, which undoubtedly
wouldn't have been scrubbed to my standards!

I enjoyed this weekly expedition, which always took
the whole morning. It got me out of the flat and
among the people, and I loved the busy, noisy bar-
gaining atmosphere. At the end of the morning the
taxi-driver collected me, took me home, and helped
me put all the bags into the lift. Upstairs the rest of the
team would unload the bags and pack away our pur-
chases, so I didn't have to carry anything except
Nathan. The worst part of the whole thing was spending an hour doing the accounts afterwards! We cooked
the food in our flat for the two families and the girls'
team, and occasionally for the boys' team, who lived
some distance away on the other side of the town.

When Nathan was about eighteen months old I found
that I was pregnant again, to everyone's delight. Curiously, it was only at this point that we discovered that
Ron and I had incompatible blood groups—Ron is

Rhesus positive and I am Rhesus negative—which often causes problems for a second pregnancy. So I had to have weekly checks and blood tests throughout the waiting period. As I was booked into a private Catholic hospital overlooking a beautiful bay, I quite enjoyed my regular trips out there. I was fit and well the whole time, and continued with my shopping expeditions right up until the last couple of weeks.

'When exactly is the baby due, Nan?' asked George one day.

'February the fourth, George,' put in Drena. 'It's in everybody's diary. You aren't trying to take Ron away then, are you?' she added suspiciously.

'No, of course not,' he replied. 'But did you realise that there's going to be a transport strike on the fifth? How is Nan going to get to hospital if the baby comes then?'

'Well, we weren't planning to take her by bus!' Drena said. 'Won't there be any taxis?'

'Nothing at all, according to the newspaper,' said George. 'We'd better make some alternative arrangements.'

'Or make sure she has the baby early,' suggested Drena.

'Oh, don't worry about me,' I said airily. 'If necessary, Ron can wheel me to the hospital on a banana cart!'

Sure enough, 4th February came and went without so much as a twinge, though I did get a bit tired of everyone watching me all the time. At four am the following morning, though, I woke up. I didn't want to disturb Ron with a false alarm, so I let him sleep on until six-thirty. By then I was sure: strike or no strike, this was going to be the day!

As no one on the OM team had a car, we had asked another missionary who lived just along the road if he would take me in to the hospital. Ron rushed off to catch him before he left for work, and returned to find the flat a hive of industry. I was trying to brush my long hair, and Drena was quickly putting my overnight things into a bag. I'd been walking around barefoot on the stone floors of the flat, and so my feet were filthy; I was determined not to go into hospital with dirty feet, but I was too big by that stage to reach them myself, so one of the girls from the team was kindly washing my feet for me!

We got to the hospital in good time, and once again Ron was able to stay for the birth. The doctor had expected the delivery to be difficult, but I was determined to have a natural birth this time.

For a while everything went well, and I concentrated on my breathing exercises, trying to work with the contractions; however, towards the end I began to tire. The baby's head was visible but I just didn't seem to have the strength in my muscles to push it out. I was screaming with each effort, but I didn't want to have to resort to those forceps again.

'Close your mouth, then,' said Ron, 'and save your strength for pushing!'

Just then he noticed something, and called to the midwife.

'Is the baby lying straight?' he asked. 'It looks as though the bulge is bigger on the left side.'

'Yes,' she replied, 'the baby's lying more on her left side, but that doesn't matter.'

'But it does,' he protested. 'Her left side is the weak side. If you pressed there with your hand, wouldn't it give her muscles some help?'

Rather taken aback at this commonsense suggestion, the midwife did as he asked, and with the second push Andrew was born.

Right from the start Andrew was different from Nathan. He was born with a smile, and needed much more cuddling and attention. The most noticeable difference was his colour: he was jaundiced (a result of the incompatibility of blood groups) and for the first few days his skin was rather a startling shade of yellow. As he grew older he played energetically and chatted non-stop—first incomprehensibly, then picking up a mixture of English and Hindi. He always drew attention with his happy disposition and blonde hair, and strangers pinched his cheeks and spoke to him wherever we went.

We stayed in the hospital for five days until Andrew's colour returned to normal, and Ron and Nathan visited us every day. I was a little apprehensive about how I would manage with two children, but once back at home we soon settled into a routine.

We had some help: an Indian came daily to wash the stone floors, and some of the time we had a cook to prepare the main meals for the whole team. There was no running water in the flat, but at night piped water ran into big barrels so that I could wash nappies each day. Fresh vegetables were delivered to the door, and so was milk—the milkman left his buffalo in the street and milked her into a big tin, into which he dipped one-litre containers. We always asked to see the big tin, to ensure that our milk hadn't been diluted with dirty water. In any case we boiled it, and I bought tinned milk for Andrew.

As time went on I found I was becoming more and more confident—not just because my grasp of the language was increasing and I was managing the boys well, but also because my physical condition had suddenly improved immensely, thanks to a new friend.

Ron had met Dr Aziz when he was doing some door-to-door work, selling books. When Ron discovered that he was a physiotherapist who had studied in California, he used that point of contact to get into further conversation. He told him all about my accident, and Doctor Aziz expressed an interest in seeing me, just in case he could help.

We went to the address he gave us, and found that it was a branch of a private hospital. Dr Aziz showed us round and examined me, and said that he thought he could certainly make my life easier if I was willing to come for treatment—he would treat me free.

I was impressed: I found him pleasant, enthusiastic and well-qualified, and I was more than willing to put myself into his hands. I was intent on improving my condition, and never content with the stage I had reached. I had never been prepared to be disabled, and was always striving for normality, trying to make the maximum use of my body. In particular, I wanted to be able to walk more steadily: I had learned to pick Nathan up and carry him on my hip, and he wound his legs around my waist to hold on, but I worried about losing my balance while carrying him.

Dr Aziz found that one of my legs was shorter than the other, and suggested a simple remedy. By the hospital entrance was a shoemaker's department, and there the technician shaved about a quarter of an inch off the sole of one of my sandals. Instantly I felt better balanced.

We arranged that I would visit the hospital each week with Drena, who would help me with the exercises as well as with the travelling; in fact, we both came to look forward to these outings as 'our day out' away from the team and the children and the housework. At first the exercises were designed to loosen the tendons in my foot, which had begun to tighten. As these took effect, my dropped left foot began to straighten out and I was able to walk more easily.

Then Dr Aziz explained that what I needed to do was to retrain my brain. Some of the muscles which an ordinary person would use were now inoperative, so my mind would have to teach new muscles to do certain actions. As we worked on this, some nerves which were damaged and deadened might come alive through work and exercise: with effort, determination and motivation I could come closer to normality.

This was the same message that I heard at Stanmore, and as before I entered into the task with great gusto. I credit Dr Aziz with much of the improvement which I have today: I learned to activate different muscles to swing my leg around and walk, or move my hand, and the increase in mobility was amazing, once I'd got the hang of it.

Because of these momentous improvements, I soon felt capable of going anywhere, though I never learned to like the Indian buses, and always took someone with me when I had to travel on them. They were always packed full to bursting point, with passengers hanging on all over them at precarious angles, and they often started moving unexpectedly, just as you were stepping on. I enjoyed train travel, though: for a period of about six months we lived with another family twenty miles outside Bombay, and we regularly had to make a long train journey to work or to visit the girls' team in the city. I did this with both boys quite confidently.

One positive benefit of living in India was that I

was surrounded daily by people in far worse plight than my own: I saw crippled beggars, women hauling emaciated children around, men on crutches. I pitied them, but identified with them at the same time; I felt that I was fortunate to have been given back so much. They were a constant reminder—if they could live in the heat, and the poor conditions, with no knowledge of God, then surely I had no right to self-pity.

Later on in our time in India I did have low periods when self-pity crept in, but these were usually short-lived. Our final year in particular was very trying, as rents kept rising and we were constantly searching for new accommodation. But even that had its bright side, since we got to know many more members of the team as we lived with different groups in different places.

Perhaps our greatest problem was our failure to achieve our aim. The purpose of our stay was to study George's leadership and be discipled by him. This tuition was planned to last for two years, but in fact we scarcely completed the first year. Only six months into the programme, two OM leaders were killed in a car accident in Poland. This left the European work seriously short of leadership, and George had to return to England and look for replacements; thereafter the Verwers spent six months of the year in Europe and six months in India.

They asked Ron and me to lead the work in India while they were away, helped by an Indian brother, Thomas Samuel, and his wife. Our desire to be learners meant learning through leadership once more.

The teams in India were growing both in number and in effectiveness, and Indians everywhere responded as our young Christians fanned out over the country. Whether Hindu, Muslim or nominally Christian, Indians were giving themselves whole-heartedly to the Christ of the New Testament. When they saw the simple lifestyle and active faith of our international teams of young people, working together in unity, it made the teachings of Jesus seem practical.

Ron travelled a great deal of the time, visiting teams to check on literature supplies, organise study programmes and deal with pastoral problems. Besides looking after the children, I was absorbed with meeting the single girls daily, praying with them as they went out to visit homes or offices. Working alongside Indians gave us new insights: when Shiela, from Kerala, took on responsibility in the office, we learned to share her concerns. Her parents had a large dowry ready for her marriage to a non-Christian, and Shiela was worried about her future. We prayed with her for many months and eventually her parents agreed to let her remain unmarried. Later Shiela married a vibrant Christian and established a lovely family.

Once, while Ron was in Europe, the boys and I travelled to the far north of India to work with a girls' team by the Ganges. We stayed in the compound of an old mission, in a tiny cottage attached to the Indian pastor's house, and fetched our own water from the village well. The pastor and his wife kept an open house, and their visitors often spilled over into our cottage: when we were not visiting homes with literature and Bibles, we were drinking tea with guests eager to meet foreigners. The children thrived and I enjoyed the opportunities to talk about God's love.

Then, one by one, each of us came down with hepatitis. The children toddled from bed to bed and the pastor's wife cared for them lovingly. We were prayed for and anointed with oil, and every member of the team recovered. Soon we were well enough to make the long train journey home, though still weak and very sick. The boys, fortunately, were hardly affected, and we returned to Bombay just as Ron arrived home with the new team. Amazingly, no one suffered from the usual lingering weakness which follows hepatitis.

Our four years in India taught us a great deal—about ourselves, our marriage, and our spiritual life. We discovered great areas of inadequacy, and found that our training was not meeting these; on the other hand, we found that we were capable of doing much more than we had expected. We learned a new language— though our three-month intensive course in Urdu was interrupted when Ron, too, suffered a bout of hepatitis, and I was torn between nursing him and caring for the boys, so we didn't get much work done then. We learned to appreciate and love the Indian people, with their openness and hospitality.

For me, the whole experience was the fulfilment of my childhood dream of working as a missionary in a needy third-world country. I found it not very different from being a missionary at home, except that it was harder work: with no modern conveniences simply surviving from day to day took up a lot of time. It was good to find that I could do this joyfully, most of the time.

Ron, too, enjoyed it and adapted well to the new conditions: he especially loved the first six months of travelling and learning.

Our marriage relationship deepened as we grew in confidence. The accident and our long separations in England had given us a rocky beginning, but now we began to appreciate and trust each other afresh. Ron came to respect my ability to manage my own life, to accept my disability while fighting to overcome it, and to run the home and be both father and mother to the boys when he was away. I loved to see his dedication to the work and his enthusiasm for every new challenge, while ensuring that the time he spent at home with the family was quality time; he always gave the boys his full attention.

I learned that we both had a role to play in mission: I had to be a buffer for his leadership. When team members didn't know how to approach Ron or were angry with him, they would often work it off on me, and expect me to communicate their feelings to Ron.

We grew spiritually, too, as we learned to trust God no matter what happened. One aspect for which I felt ill-prepared was the atmosphere of spiritual darkness which surrounded us in that society; it felt like a spiritual vacuum, which frightened me.

One event in particular recalls that nameless menace which I sometimes felt. Ron went to a Salvation Army meeting and brought home with him a contact he had made: the man had asked him for money for food, and Ron refused, but invited him home for a meal.

As the man ate, he talked, and addressed himself mainly to me. He kept eyeing me and watching my every move until I felt almost as though I was being hypnotised and drawn inside him. With an enormous effort I got up and went into the bedroom: I found that I was shaking all over. Ron followed me and asked what was wrong, but I didn't know—I just felt that the man had some evil intent towards me, and I needed to pray. By the time Ron had fetched one of the girls to sit with me, I was quite calm; no one quite understood what had happened, but they asked the man to leave.

At first, Ron sometimes thought I was imagining such spiritual attacks, but I was certain that we had met with the powers of darkness, which could only be cast down by claiming the power of the risen Lord Jesus. And after a while he agreed that at certain times I did seem to have a heightened spiritual discernment, both an awareness of evil and an understanding of people's problems, and my feelings usually proved to be accurate.

In many ways, living in India permanently changed our outlook on life. We often find it difficult, even now, to live in the West; we miss the flexibility, the communal spirit, and the simplicity of India. Sometimes we find it hard to appreciate the attitudes of Western Christians; some groups seem to place a special emphasis on certain activities like healing and spiritual warfare, as though no one ever practised them before. In India, living as we did among Hinduism and folk religion, we were used to seeing people possessed by powerful spirits. Similarly, in the absence of good medical care in a country where disease was rife, we always had to trust God for healing and protection. We didn't see any need to make a fuss about this; it's so easy to concentrate on the more spectacular gifts of the spirit at the expense of looking for the fruits. It's harder to pray for patience, faithfulness, gentleness and self-control.

Looking back, I sometimes wonder how we survived those years, but our various hardships seemed normal in the context of life out there. The climate was hot, humid and sticky—in the monsoons, it rained so hard that you could hardly see across the street. The heat was enervating, and the smallest activity would leave you bathed in sweat. Yet we thrived, and the boys grew up in perfect health. I ensured that they ate a conventional Western diet, as far as possible, but Ron and I wanted to identify with the Indian people, so we lived and ate as the Indians did. What we failed to recognise was that in fact the diet and the unfamiliar climate were very debilitating; we were both being worn down by it as surely as a rock is worn down by dripping water.

We often had to pull foreigners off the travelling teams and rebuild them with Western food. Their bodies simply could not take the diet and lifestyle they were sharing with the Indian brothers they worked alongside. It was easy to be critical of the old-style missionaries who lived in compounds, separate from the ordinary people. Yet having seen the poverty and disease of India, we came to realise that was probably the only way to survive long-term missionary work.

We were hard on ourselves and on those working under us: we expected the best from ourselves, and though we tried to understand other people's weaknesses, sometimes it was difficult to live with them. There were many subcultures within the team, which included young people from several European countries as well as the US and India; we wanted to live in unity, and effectively, but we disregarded the inevitable stresses this brought.

It wasn't until we moved out of Bombay to the suburbs, away from the immediacy of city life and the team environment, that we realised that we were both falling apart. I was tired out with everyday existence, constantly battling with my physical handicaps. Ron was worn out by the increasing responsibilities of administration and organisation. And we were both weary of trying to cope with the growing work and the difficulties of preserving unity in the team.

The last six months were uninspiring ones of grinding routine. Much though we had loved India, it was a relief when the time came for us to leave: we felt that we needed a long holiday, and we were looking forward to travelling back to England. At last we could put all our problems behind us and relax for a while.

What did happen next was a surprise to both of us.

Chapter 8

We were looking forward to a real rest after our years in India. So, typically, we planned for our return to Europe the kind of journey most people would undertake once in a lifetime, and then only if at the peak of fitness—and never with two small children.

We took a boat from Bombay to Karachi in suffocating heat, and then a train from Karachi to Iran. At Quetta (still in Pakistan) a group of Afghans got on the train and stuffed sacks of herbs under the seats of our compartment; it was only when we heard them bribing the guards to let them travel that we realised that the sacks contained hashish.

From Pakistan we travelled on overland through Iran, staying for a few days with friends in Tehran, and going on across northern Iran to the Turkish border. We crossed the Turkish mountains in a rattling old bus, twisting and turning on the roughly asphalted roads which took a corkscrew route through the passes. I was immensely relieved when we reached Istanbul, because the rest of our journey to Belgium was to be by train—and of necessity that route would have to be flat, and fairly straight!

I loved the travelling: I enjoyed the stimulus of

133

seeing new places, new faces every day, getting a taste of each country we passed through at stations and rest stops. It wasn't very comfortable, of course; I got very tired, and the boys were rather a handful: aged fifteen months and three years, they didn't much like having to sit still. But it was great to be on our own as a family again, sharing an adventure.

We arrived in Zaventem, near Brussels, in time for the OM annual conference. In the first week of July some 350 young people (mainly from the US and Europe) arrived for a week of training; they were then divided into teams and went out to various countries for three weeks before moving on to their placements. Meanwhile the leaders who went out with them returned to Zaventem in the first week of August to repeat the process with a second group, this time mainly European.

Ron, the boys and I shared a single room with a balcony, overlooking a garage workshop where the OM vehicles were overhauled. While Ron chose and organised the teams of young people, leading sessions on language, culture, and Bible training, I looked after the children and helped in the nursery. At the end of the first week, Ron went off to northern France with a team, while I stayed behind. Most of my free time was spent writing letters: I was trying to organise a reunion of the team who had just spent four years in India, and I also needed to send out a newsletter to all the people who supported us personally with prayer and finance.

Somehow the pace never seemed to let up; I always felt tired, and I seemed to need more and more hours of sleep, but still no warning bells sounded in my head. I was doing as much as many of the able-bodied team members, and I was glad when Ron returned from France for the August conference—at least he would share the burden of looking after the children.

The end, when it came, was sudden; the decline rapid. Towards the end of the conference week we held a night of extended prayer, which was a regular feature of OM events. I was fine then, though the next day I remember feeling unusually tired, like a clock running down. I skipped the teaching session I had planned to attend, and went back to our room to be alone. That evening Ron looked in as I was preparing for bed, to say that he was going out to pick up some books, and would be back in about an hour. The boys were asleep on a mattress on the floor of our room.

I sat on the bed in my nightie and felt a great wave of fear engulf me. I was sure Ron was in great danger; he was going to be killed. I couldn't remember where he was, and I went out into the corridor to look for him. On my way I passed the door of the next room, where a young couple were staying: the husband was West Indian, the wife English. Once again I was overwhelmed with irrational fears, this time out of my childhood in the racist Deep South of the United States. Ideas I have never personally subscribed to came rushing into my head, things I had heard people say when I was a child: what was a white woman doing married to a black man? It was wrong, unnatural. I was afraid to go back into my room, next to theirs. And where was Ron? And where were my children? I didn't know, I couldn't remember; I was fighting against a great tide of fear and weariness; I wanted to lie down in the corridor and sleep.

Fortunately, at that moment Drena came along. She was surprised to see me wandering in the corridor in my nightie, but quickly realised that I was confused, almost delirious. She got me back to bed and ran for George, her husband.

'Come quick,' she panted. 'Something's wrong with Nan. You've got to find Ron for her, she's terribly frightened and muddled. I'll have to go back and look after her.'

By the time Ron returned I was almost hysterical, talking wildly and making no sense at all. Drena hoped his presence would calm me, but she was disappointed.

I didn't recognise him.

Someone must have sedated me, because I can remember very little after that. I have a hazy recollection of travelling on a boat, with Ron's face bending over me as he helped me onto a bunk. He looked haggard with worry. The boys were on another bunk nearby, but I felt no interest in them. All I wanted to do was sleep again.

Ron had found someone to take us to his Aunt Dolf's house in Chelsfield when we arrived in England, but I knew nothing of the journey, except that I could hardly walk. Someone carried our luggage for us, someone else looked after the boys. Aunt Dolf was horrified when she opened the door and saw us standing there: Ron half carried me up the stairs and put me to bed.

To begin with, everyone hoped that a good rest would put me right, but the GP who came to see me was doubtful. After two days I was still sleeping most of the time, but when I was awake I recognised no one. I was living in a nightmare, where dream figures came and went in a strange room.

The GP made arrangements for me to be admitted to a mental hospital in Maidstone.

Once again my recollections are hazy: a huge room with fifty or so beds in it; women talking, singing, mumbling; women shambling along a corridor, muttering; someone dancing, and being restrained by a nurse. I didn't want to stay here; I was shouting, screaming, fighting; Ron carried me to a bed and held me down. I saw Dolf's face, with tears streaming as she turned away from my bed; Ron holding my hand as yet another needle was slipped into my arm and the merciful black drugged sleep took everything away.

I was sedated, heavily. Ron and Dolf visited me, but I didn't know it. They brought the boys, and I was allowed to walk to the door and look at them: two small children playing in a corridor, with a woman looking after them. I wasn't even interested.

At last, one visiting time, the doctor stood by my bed.

'Mr George, I don't think your wife is going to respond to the drug treatment. I suggest ECT—electro-convulsive therapy—is probably the best thing to try. It often has very good results. But we need your signature...'

Ron looked across at me as I sat on the side of the bed, but I wasn't listening; I was staring vacantly at the wall.

Ron sighed. 'All right. Anything, if you think it might help.'

When I was in the Stanmore Orthopaedic Hospital I had had electric shock treatment on my arms, in an attempt to stimulate the nerves. So when the doctor explained that they were going to attach electrodes to my head, I wasn't at all worried. It had been done to my arms, why not my head? In any case, I didn't mind what happened to me—I was in a perpetual daze.

I had three separate treatments on different days; the first two had no effect at all. After the third treatment I opened my eyes and looked around me. The fog had cleared. I knew where I was. My mind felt fresh and alert, and I immediately buttonholed the unsuspecting nurse who was removing the electrodes.

'Look here, nurse, I feel fine. How long are they going to keep me in here? When will my husband be coming in? How are my children? Where is that doctor? I've a lot of questions I want to ask him!'

Ron and I had a long session with the doctor that evening. Ron's eyes were shining as he looked at me: he could hardly believe the transformation. My blank, zombie-like expression had disappeared. I sat holding his hand, longing to say how sorry I was to have put him through all this, but I still felt too fragile. I wanted to know exactly what had happened to me: how had my mind collapsed?

The doctor asked us to recall the events leading up to my breakdown, and as we did so, I was appalled to see what we had done. How could we have been so stupid, how could we have driven ourselves so hard? Some of what Ron said was hard for me to hear. I had been aggressive, irritable; on the channel ferry I had thrown away the tranquillisers I'd been given, and refused to have Ron near me. I shivered—the nightmare didn't seem very far away, even now.

'Well,' said the doctor, when we had finished, 'I think a pattern emerges from all that, don't you? You are clearly suffering from malnutrition; the diet in India wasn't adequate for you, especially after having two children. And you don't seem to have accepted the limitations of your disability: you have been push-ing and pushing your body much harder than you should. It simply doesn't want to co-operate with you any more! Tell me, if this hadn't happened, would you have stopped working this summer?'

'No, I guess not,' I replied. 'I mean, you never stop working with small children anyway, but I would have gone on working for OM as well.'

'There you are, then,' he smiled. 'You are fitted with a safety mechanism: you overloaded the system, and it forced you to stop.'

'There is one thing,' I said hesitantly. 'I did have a sort of breakdown years ago, when I was at Bible College. I was working to put myself through college, doing my regular courses, counselling, leading Bible studies—just taking on too much, I suppose. I got over it with rest and some medical help, but I dropped out of college for a while.'

'Well, that's what you need this time, too: rest and some medication. We'll have to see that you get it.'

'But when will I be allowed to leave hospital?' I asked. 'I want to get back to my family.'

The doctor looked at my notes. 'Now that you are feeling better,' he said, 'I think our main concern must be your weight. If you can get your weight up to nine stone, then I think we can safely discharge you.'

Ron and I were delighted; I've always had a prob-lem with my weight, but in the past it was usually keeping it down! I was sure that I could quickly put on the fourteen pounds or so I needed to 'earn' my discharge. I applied myself to some serious eating.

Meanwhile I still had time to kill on the ward, and it was a disturbing place. It was impossible to reach many of the women with normal conversation: as I had been, they were withdrawn from the world or drugged into oblivion. I peered nervously into what were called 'private rooms' but which I soon saw to be padded cells.

Left to myself, I considered my position. Clearly something had gone wrong with my brain: was it really all right again? How could I prove to myself that I could still think? I concentrated on verses I had memorised from the Bible, which comforted me doubly—not only because I was able to remember them, but also because I felt they had a 'washing' power which cleansed my mind of the terrors and nightmares which had governed it.

When Ron visited me, we talked about the doctor's diagnosis. He was right about the malnutrition, and about my pushing my poor inadequate and broken body beyond its limits—but he didn't know the half of it! We looked back on the final months of our time in India, at the emotional conflicts, the personality clashes, the struggle to keep the teams working in unity. We thought of the spiritual draining, the constant giving out to children, other missionaries, and the ordinary people; we thought of the atmosphere of spiritual warfare in which we had lived, with a Hindu temple underneath our flat and idols on every street corner. How wise is God who decrees that man should labour and then rest—and how foolish we had been not to take the rest we so desperately needed.

We each had faults to confess to the other. I knew that I had allowed resentments to build up in my heart: when Ron was working so hard I was concerned for his well-being, but also for my own—I was jealous of the work which consumed all his energies, leaving less and less for me and the boys. Ron, in his turn, recognised that he had become immersed in his work and relied too much on my unhesitating willingness to shoulder the responsibility for the family, and support him. It seemed oddly familiar, as we sat there on my hospital bed, holding hands and faced by crisis. Once again we had to reassess our marriage and our roles within it. What did we expect of ourselves and each other?

Meanwhile, the first priority was my release. I rested. I ate. And I ate some more. By September I weighed nine stones, and was allowed to go home to Chelsfield, to the loving concern of Auntie Dolf, and the vague disapproval of Uncle Tom, who thought our whole lifestyle was dangerously irresponsible, and wished we would just settle down tidily in Kent with sensible jobs.

We did settle down—for a whole month. Then we decided to go and visit my parents in the US.

Initially we planned it just as a family visit; my parents were longing to see their grandsons, and they were eager to see me, too. I was afraid I would be rather a shock to them—after all, I had left the US single, carefree and energetic; I returned married, with children, and disabled. I felt that I needed to get to know my parents afresh, as an adult—and I know my mother wanted to nurse me.

In addition, we wanted counsel and advice. We had many faithful supporters in the States and we felt we should report to them about our activities, though I had shirked the issue in our last newsletter. I said that I had just come out of hospital, but didn't give any details of my mental breakdown. I felt ashamed and confused by what had happened to me. Surely Christians shouldn't just collapse in that way? Weren't we supposed to have a support in God which would uphold us under stress? I had to think through all these things, and I realised that my mother's particular brand of commonsense caring would help me to do so.

In fact the answers to these questions took some months to emerge. My mother was concerned about the enormous quantities of drugs I was still taking, and I realised that I was becoming dependent on the tranquillisers and other medication prescribed for me by the hospital. Gradually and with much effort I managed to reduce the dose, and eventually I discarded them entirely. I prayed at length for help in this, and for understanding of why it had all happened.

It was my mother who gave me the clue: one day she said, 'A teachable spirit is the best asset you can have.'

Then I realised that I'd been asking the wrong questions. It shouldn't be, 'Why did God allow this to happen?' but 'I did this. What can I learn from it?' It took some time for me to stop feeling guilty and inadequate, though: I realised that to survive an accident like mine was generally regarded as an evidence of spiritual strength, while to have a mental breakdown was seen as weakness. There are even second-class illnesses!

My parents helped us to find a house, and Ron decided he wanted to be involved with a local church which had no pastor. It was the first time we'd had the chance to enjoy a church fellowship as a family, because we'd always been out on the mission field, and it was wonderful. Before we knew it we were teaching in the Sunday school and running the youth group. We were still being supported by our many prayer partners, and we felt we owed it to them to keep working.

In the past we had always worked with young people of college age, but now we were involved with teenagers who were growing up fast. It was challenging work: if the teens were dissatisfied with life, they were so vulnerable to outside pressures. The drug culture, in particular, was new since I had last lived in California.

There was one girl who sometimes came to church, though she was not a Christian. Gail was depressed and angry by turns; she had tried everything—sex, drugs, danger—but nothing satisfied or had any meaning for her. She was living with her boyfriend and addicted to drugs, and her life was one of emotional torment. She wanted to commit suicide but she was afraid.

I spent long hours talking with her, and I think she realised how closely I identified with her distress. I, too, had until recently been dependent on drugs; I, too, had wrestled with the emotional hurricanes of depression, frustration and anger. But I had God as my base: knowing that Christ had suffered as I had suffered, that he was tempted as we were tempted, enabled me to go on. God comforted me, and in some way I was able to pass on that comfort to Gail, even though she didn't yet know the Saviour.

My dealings with Gail began to shed more light on the confusion I felt about my breakdown. In the past I had often been impatient with other people's weaknesses; had God allowed my suffering to make me more sensitive to others' needs? Ron pointed me to a passage in Corinthians:

Praise be to the God and Father of our Lord Jesus Christ, the Father of compassion and the God of all comfort, who comforts us in all our troubles, so that we can comfort those in any trouble with the comfort we ourselves have received from God. For just as the sufferings of Christ flow over into our lives, so also through Christ our comfort overflows (2 Cor 1:3–5).

I recalled once, long ago, praying, 'O Lord, disturb me.' I had wanted God to come into my life and do his work, to change me and make me his own. I didn't understand then what the cost might be. Yet here I was, slowly but surely being changed, learning patience and sympathy. It was almost as if the pressure of pain or temptation was necessary for each stage in my growth and development.

Meanwhile our work went on. Ron, not being an American citizen, had to leave the country every three months to preserve his 'visitor' status, so after a while he decided to take a trip to Mexico, and take some of our youth group with him. They could experience a different culture which was very close at hand, and do some evangelistic work. Shortly before the trip was due to happen we realised that there would be an OM conference in Milwaukee (half way across the States from California) and we thought that this would be a wonderful preparation for our young people.

We bought an old school bus to travel in. Just before we left we were told that it was illegal to drive one of these bright yellow buses if it was not being used as a school bus, so friends at church painted it white overnight! Ron set off with the youth group, and I went with the boys and my parents to visit my sister; we would meet the bus later.

Unfortunately, our car was involved in a collision. My mother was badly hurt, I was knocked unconscious and Nathan bit his tongue nearly off. Only my father and Andrew emerged unscathed. We were kept in hospital for a couple of days and then released, and poor Ron left the kids at the conference while he came to collect us from the hospital.

Probably at that point I should have gone quietly home to recover, but I couldn't bear to be left out of the action. I refused to be beaten: I'd planned to go with Ron on this trip, and I was determined to do so. My stubbornness came to the fore, and with it my ability to make mistakes—the same ones, all over again. Still suffering from shock I went on to the conference, where we taught, led meetings, and joined in the night of extended prayer. Then we drove through the night to Texas, with a bus load of excited teenagers and our two little boys.

By this time I was tired and irritable, and Ron, recognising the warning signs, persuaded me to go home for a rest. Dad collected me from the airport and I stayed at home for a few days, resting and eating. But I was anxious to get back to Ron; I knew he couldn't be expected to manage the children as well as the responsibility for the teenagers. And, as before, I couldn't bear the thought that my life had to slow down, while his went on without me.

At the end of the week I flew back to Mexico City, assuring Ron that I was fit and well. So he drove down to southern Mexico with a team of boys, while I stayed with the children and a girls' team in the city. I enjoyed giving the girls a taste of mission, witnessing for Christ outside their own culture, and I enjoyed the lifestyle: the culture, the food, even the temperament of the people all reminded me of India.

I was working at full stretch, supervising a team of young girls, keeping house and looking after the children, and the tell-tale tiredness began to creep up on me. I felt it coming but I couldn't give up: my pride wouldn't let me. I was sure I could keep going for just a few more days until Ron got back.

Once again the end came suddenly. I went out shopping, leaving the boys with a babysitter, and somehow managed to get lost—perhaps the confusion was already beginning. I asked directions from a man who offered me a lift in his car, but instead of taking me home he took me to a local park.

I don't think his intentions were very sinister: he tried to put his arms around me but there was no question of rape. Nevertheless I felt dirty, scared and ashamed, and I broke away from him, screaming and sobbing. He didn't try to follow me; I wandered the streets for hours until at last I found my way home. The babysitter was alarmed and telephoned for Ron, who drove back immediately. By the time he arrived, late that night, I was once again lost in the nightmare of exhaustion and terror that had surrounded me before.

Ron realised, this time, that there was no question of just resting: he took me straight to the local hospital.

When I opened my eyes I saw a yellow, stained-looking ceiling. I lifted my arm to shield my eyes from the harsh light, and saw a plastic identity bracelet on my wrist. I had a spasm of panic: where was I? Was I back in the hospital in Yugoslavia? I squirmed on the bed and realised, with relief, that I could move. I rolled on to my side and looked around.

I was in a tiny cell: one wall consisted only of metal bars, with a locked door in it. My bed was a mattress on the floor; in the other corner of the floor was a hole—from the smell I could tell it was a primitive toilet. 'Oh, God,' I thought silently, 'what have I done now?'

I sat in that solitary room for hours; once a nurse brought me some food; once I was given an injection that made me sleep. After what seemed like days, I heard a jangling of keys and a familiar voice, and Ron came in. He knelt by my side and I fell into his arms.

'Where am I?' I asked. 'Am I in prison? What's been happening to me?'

'It's all right, Nan,' he said soothingly. 'You just need two or three days' care, that's all.'

'I want to go home,' I said, trying to control the panic in my voice. 'I'll be all right if I can go home.'

'I'm sorry, Nan,' he answered. 'I didn't think it would be like this. It's just an ordinary hospital, not a prison. It's a special ward...'

His voice tailed away as the nurse returned. She was carrying yet another syringe.

After three days I was discharged, slightly groggy with the drugs, but calm and in my right mind. We collected the team together and drove back across Mexico and Texas to California, as if nothing had happened. We didn't tell the teenagers about the special ward; they thought I'd just had to have some routine treatment in hospital.

When we got home we settled into a routine; I looked after the children and the house, while Ron travelled, doing evangelistic work, and helped at the local church. I needed time to recover my balance, to feel secure, and I knew that a period of quiet house-keeping was the answer.

Everyone has a finite amount of energy each day. My trouble was that I wanted to do as much as everyone else, forgetting that my energy store was already depleted: everything—getting up from a chair, walking, getting dressed—was a greater effort for me than for other people. Now I could look back and see a pattern of peaks and troughs: when I felt well I worked hard, but I disliked stability and routine, and could never resist working on, travelling and meeting people, when I should have been resting. I went on stubbornly, refusing to give in to my disability, until exhaustion claimed not only my body but my mind.

Even I could see that wasn't God's will for me; somehow I had to adjust my expectations. It was hard to have to face the fact that I wasn't superwoman, and I took the problem to God in prayer. I was open and honest, admitting that I didn't want to do his will. I felt like Jacob, wrestling with the angel until he touched the innermost part of his soul; the breaking of my obstinate will could be done by God alone.

There was no miraculous peace for me after this, no saintly acquiescence, no transformation from Martha to Mary. I still have dark days of depression and discouragement, when my body refuses to respond to my mind and frustration spills over. But the family are very patient with me. They realise, now, that I'll sort things out in time, and that once again I have to wrestle with God before I come to surrender and have peace.

We spent two years in America before returning to England; then we were offered a house in London by the London City Mission, in association with OM, doing work called 'experimental evangelism'. It meant outreach in every possible way, trying to contact the people in our part of Camberwell Green.

We had a team of three girls living with us, and

together we set about penetrating a culture as alien to me as that of India. Nathan was attending the local primary school, and Andrew was at playgroup, so I had lots of opportunities to talk to other mothers at the school gate. We kept open house, welcoming everyone who came: in the evenings the house was always full of young people, mostly skinheads. I would escape upstairs to put the children to bed, and when I came down again the living-room carpet was always covered in cigarette ash.

We suffered all the stresses of inner-city life associated with urban mission; Ron loved it, being a Londoner at heart, but I found it less easy to settle in, foreigner that I was. On one occasion I came home from a coffee morning and said to Ron, 'What is the Great Train Robbery?'

Ron explained about the robbery which had happened several years previously.

'Oh,' I replied. 'I only wondered, because there were two women there today who said their husbands were in prison for taking part in it!'

The work went well: we ran an art exhibition, with a competition for local schools, and a rock concert which drew in many of the local skinheads. But most of all we provided somewhere for the youngsters to go in the evenings, and someone for them to relate to.

However, I still had problems with my role. I was careful not to overstretch my meagre resources again: thus far, at least, I had learned my lesson. But I was frustrated to find that what energy I had was always expended on the mundane work of running the house. I didn't mind looking after my family—that, after all, was my God-given responsibility—but I resented running a hostel for the girls on the team. I didn't want to be a house-mother, and I felt the girls needed to become domesticated, too, and able to fend for themselves. I seemed to cook thousands of meals, tidy everyone's rooms, and clean the hard-worked living-room over and over again. I wanted to join in the work of evangelism, the street witnessing and singing, as the girls did, but I seemed always confined by my domestic duties.

Naturally, this frustration boiled over into my relationship with Ron, and we had many arguments. I was envious of the freedom enjoyed by the girls in the team, who had no family responsibilities, and I envied Ron, too, his comparative freedom to work. However, Ron was entering a dark period of his own. He always felt restless while in England; the London culture wasn't new to him as it had been to me, and it offered him little challenge. He was suffering from a kind of burn-out, an emotional exhaustion, and he didn't even want to go to church. I needed the family fellowship of a church, and was amazed at Ron's reluctance to be involved—I'd never seen him like this before. He still felt the need for further training and intellectual stimulus, and realised that in OM he was not going to find what he wanted. At the end of the year we resigned from OM.

As if to confirm our decision, almost immediately Ron was offered work as pastor of a tiny church in Romford. It was the ideal solution: outside London, to give us all a breathing space from urban stress; a three-bedroomed council house, which was like a dream compared with our earlier living conditions; and since the church was on a council estate taking overspill from East London, the work was largely with the same kind of people as those we had lived among for the past year.

Nathan and Andrew enjoyed the fresh air and the freedom; I enjoyed being a pastor's wife; Ron enjoyed the pastoral work, and the study necessary for reading God's word and teaching it. We had six months which felt just like a holiday, until OM contacted us. Would we be willing to return to our original missionary work? They wanted us to go to Iran. They were looking for workers who were experienced in overseas situations and who were able to relate sensitively to Islamic culture: our four years in India and one previous year in Iran made us ideal candidates.

Chapter 9

Our responses to this call from OM were very different. Ron's was one of caution: he had no inclination, he said, to go abroad again merely for the sake of it; he would consider going only if there was some specific goal to achieve. Mine was one of horror: I was willing to go anywhere for God—but not there! My memories of our year in Iran, before my accident, were not particularly happy, in spite of our engagement and marriage. I had found the language complex to learn, the people difficult to reach, and the restrictions placed on women in a Muslim culture hard to accept.

I struggled for obedience, but I didn't want to go. Could God really be leading us back to where we started, in Iran, after all we'd been through?

We knew, though, from our contacts who were still living in Iran, that the old order was changing: the Shah had been bringing in reforms which had altered the nature of the country faster than anyone would have thought possible. In the end we made an arrangement with OM: Ron would go out for three weeks to assess the situation. Although I knew he didn't share my sense of dread that God might lead us back, I trusted him to understand the difficulties I'd had with the restricted life out there, and to look carefully at all aspects of the work. While he was away I ran a Vacation Bible School in our little church.

It was a hot afternoon in August when Ron rang from the airport to say he was on his way home. I remember putting the boys to bed, and then sitting outside on the front step in the long summer evening, waiting for him. At last I saw him turn the corner and walk along the pavement towards me, and I could see from the spring in his step that the answer was positive.

'O Lord,' I prayed silently, 'give me grace.'

Over a meal that evening Ron outlined his plans.

'We must have a clear aim,' he said, 'and one that can be accomplished in a three- or four-year term. First of all we'll have to get a job out there, preferably with the British Council, so that we can get work permits. Then, once we're there, we'll set up a Christian book agency, to import and sell Christian books. Once the agency is set up, it will generate jobs, which will enable a whole series of people to go out there and work.'

'That's a great idea,' I answered. 'It was OK in India—the British could work there without a work permit. But when we were in Iran I hated having to leave the country for a few days every three months, just because we were only there on tourist visas. I always thought that was bad for family and team life. But how are you going to get a job in the first place?'

'Oh, that's all sorted out,' he said. 'I think the British Council is going to offer me a job teaching Business English—no, Nan, don't laugh like that!

You'll just have to help me with correcting essays, that's all!'

Even with Ron's appalling inability to write good English, it looked as though we were going.

It cost me a struggle to give up my role as a pastor's wife and return to Iran. The six months in Romford had been a time of refreshment for all of us, and for me especially. I'd built up close relationships with my neighbours, whose children played in our garden while the mums chatted over coffee: it was good to be free of the smoke and grime of London, free of worry about the boys playing in the street (Andrew had been shot by an air rifle outside our house in Camberwell). Now I was being asked to give up my green pastures and follow my husband's enthusiasm for overseas mission. I knew it was a God-given, guided enthusiasm, but that didn't make it any easier. It brought me up against another aspect of the breaking of my will: was I really able to call my husband 'lord' and let him be the head of the family? Was I willing to give up my desire to do what I wanted in a place where I felt secure and at ease, to follow him abroad?

When I was single I'd always wanted to be independent, to make my own decisions. I sometimes wonder how stormy our marriage might have been if my accident hadn't happened, because that event forced me to accept help and to recognise that I was no longer in sole charge of my own life: as a married couple we would have to be interdependent, sharing the decision-making. Once I had adapted to marriage and motherhood I realised that I had to create a structure so that the family could function, and like most women I spent much of my time considering the needs of my husband and children before my own.

In a way, that made it harder. I had so little freedom these days: was even that to be taken away from
me? I had a forlorn sense of forsaking a way of life I
found satisfying and fulfilling. Ron wasn't a domineer-
ing husband, trying to suppress me. I knew that when
we married I had placed myself not just in submis-
sion, but under his protection—and on how many
occasions I had been glad of it! How many hospital
wards had he paced, under pressure of the bond of
being married to me? Now the pressure was on me—
would I bring myself under his headship and go
cheerfully by his side?

I managed it all—except, perhaps, the cheerful
part.

All the arrangements went like clockwork, and by the
end of the year we found ourselves established in
Tehran once more. Our living conditions were wonderful: we rented a semi-basement flat in a huge house
at the end of an alley. Our windows looked out on a
traditional paved Persian garden, with flower beds,
shady trees, and a pool. The boys were allowed to play
in this walled garden with the three children who lived
upstairs, as our landlord was keen for them to learn
some English, and of course Andrew and Nathan
picked up Farsi with an ease that put me to shame.

Ron's teaching at the British Council wasn't a full-
time job, so when he had finished marking exercises
with my help, he was able to begin the work of setting
up the book agency. The boys were enrolled in the
International School and loved their long days there:
they left the house at 6.45 am to be picked up by the
school bus, and returned at around 4.30 pm.

Ashraf, our landlord's wife, became like a sister to
me; we spent time together every day. She showed me

the best local shops, shared her favourite recipes, and introduced me to her friends. Best of all, she helped me with my halting attempts to communicate in her language, so that with her encouragement and my regular lessons at the Iran-American Society, I was soon able to make myself understood. It was important to be able to speak the language: English was not respected in Iran as it was in India, and I had to set a good example to the OM team members who were working in Tehran.

We dined, Persian style, with Ashraf and her husband, who was a lawyer, and they taught us how to behave in company. For a start it's polite to arrive late, bringing a small gift for the hosts, and you expect to spend three or four hours on such a visit. I would spend the time with Ashraf and her daughter in the kitchen, preparing the meal, while the men and boys chatted in the living room. Ashraf's children all attended different schools: one son went to an Arabic school, the other to an English Presbyterian school, and her daughter to a French Catholic school. It made for a cosmopolitan kind of household, to say the least, and meant that our landlord, Dr Ahlevi, was in touch with several different communities within Tehran.

One bonus of this was that somehow Dr Ahlevi managed to get us tickets for the Shah's birthday celebrations, which were held in a big stadium in the city. We sat close to the Royal Box, and saw the Shah and the Empress. We watched Iranian wrestling, displays by the girl scouts, traditional dancing by all the different people groups, army bands—every possible part of the culture was represented.

The family took us under their wing completely. When Ron was away on long trips they hovered over me solicitously, checking up that I was well, and bringing me khoresh—a dish made of spinach and other greens—as a gift. The houses were all built so that they overlooked each other, anyway, and I always felt perfectly safe when I was left alone with the children.

Ashraf had found us an old Iranian lady who came in once a week to help with the heavy work around the house, and I looked forward to her Tuesday visits. I cooked a meal for her and talked to her in Farsi; I was beginning to immerse myself in the Persian culture. Our kutcheh, or alley, had houses on both sides, and soon I had friends all along it.

Once I had made these contacts, and my language ability began to improve, I felt better: my misery at returning to Iran was dispelled. I still missed my life in England, but at least I was content to be where I was.

Our house was right in the centre of Tehran, within walking distance of the shops, and close to both the men's and the women's team houses. Although Ron had an official teaching job, we still had to supervise the OM teams. It was difficult to see how to do so without disrupting our family life too much, but in the end we hit on the idea of inviting various team members to our home for breakfast, after the boys had gone off to school.

It was at one of these meetings, over the coffee and rolls, that we realised that we were ready to begin the final stage of the work: setting up the book agency. David, a young salesman who worked on the team, came in carrying a large folder of papers. He swept aside the plates on the table, and dumped them down in front of Ron.

'There you are,' he said cheerfully, 'enough orders to keep you going for a year!'

'What do you mean?' Ron asked. 'Orders from whom?'

'Well,' said David, 'you know the team have already been selling books through the churches, just as a service to local Christians. The first half of these are our ordinary orders from those churches. But our aim, after all, is to set up the whole enterprise on a larger scale. So while I've been visiting churches in the provinces to find out what books they want to buy, I've also been into all the secular bookshops in those towns. Now that the regime here is so relaxed, I don't see why we shouldn't be able to sell Christian books openly in the shops.'

Ron flicked through the sheaf of papers eagerly. 'And these are orders from bookshops?' he inquired.

'Not just that,' David replied. 'I thought we might have book-racks in other places—you know, super-markets and chemists—for our books. We'd have to service them and deliver stocks regularly, but they'd be just for our use. Then we'd have Christian books available in all sorts of outlets. I don't have many firm orders yet, but there are a dozen or so shops who've agreed to give us space when we're ready.'

He sat back with a triumphant grin and drained his coffee cup.

'I think we're about ready to go. What's the next step?'

Ron looked thoughtful. 'We'll have to get two solic-itors—one Iranian, one English—to set up the legal side of the operation. I guess that will take quite a while. Meanwhile, we'll need staff, premises—'

'Surely we won't need a shop,' I put in. 'It's going to be a distribution service, not a bookshop.'

'True,' agreed David. 'What about a flat somewhere?

We'll need somewhere to store our supplies, and some sort of office accommodation.'

'I'll look for that,' I volunteered. 'I've quite a lot of contacts, these days.'

'Right,' said Ron. 'It looks as if we're on the way!'

While these things were happening, the rest of the team was engaged in various kinds of evangelism, but they all visited churches to advertise our services, too. Even before the book agency was properly established, we found we were handling the sales of more and more Christian books. Now that the boys were both at school I decided it was time for me to do a little more to help out, and so I undertook the book-keeping. I had enough Farsi now to communicate with our Iranian banker, who came out at lunchtime sometimes to help me to tackle double-entry book-keeping in two languages!

The rest of my time was taken up simply with housekeeping: I shopped daily rather than weekly, because there were no convenience foods available, and nothing frozen. If I bought a chicken for supper it might have been plucked, but that was all—I had to clean and gut it before cooking. We bought bread fresh for each meal, which meant visiting the bakery several times a day, and sometimes I bought unbaked dough to make my own bread and pizza bases.

As well as his work for the British Council and our book company, Ron travelled a great deal meeting church leaders in the provinces, discovering what help they needed. I had responsibility for training the girls who had just come out to Iran, because they often had special problems in adapting to the Muslim culture. By that time (1973) most of the Iranian women wore Western clothes, so our girls could do the same, but still their dress had to be moderate, with elbows and legs well covered. It was too easy for them to give the wrong impression to Iranian men.

'What a man in the West thinks about a woman, a man in the East does,' I warned them. It was true—in shops they would be touched and fondled, and crushed unnecessarily on buses. The men would do this only to Western women, about whom they had doubtless heard wild stories of loose morals, but never to the women of their own culture. I taught the girls always to travel in twos, and generally to carry a stick. When they were stared at on buses I told them to say loudly, 'Don't you have a sister at home to look at?'— a suggestion which usually embarrassed the offender. I wanted the girls' time in Iran to be fruitful, which meant that it was important that they were not offended or scared, and neither were they offensive to the Iranians.

Often we held tea parties so that Iranian women would visit the girls' team house. Hospitality was vitally important, and we always had lots of people coming in for meals—mainly lunch and breakfast, so that our own family life didn't suffer. These were new skills for the girls to learn, too, for they came from Western European cultures where often the home is downgraded, and becomes just a place where people 'tank up and take off'. The girls had to learn that in the East the traditions of hospitality exalt the home to a central role, a place worthy of the exercise of all your intellect and ministering skills. Here it could be a centre of witness.

As I began to teach the girls this, I suddenly saw its relevance to my own life. All my experiences of the last few years swam into focus, as I realised that far from hating this time in Iran as I had expected, I found myself busy, fulfilled, and happy. How had I come to love this country so much, when my previous visit had been so unsatisfactory?

Most of my difficulties, it seemed to me, came about through my desire to be dynamic, working actively for God. Some of my stubbornness had been useful to me, driving me to recover from the accident and strive towards a normal life, but much of it had been destructive. My refusal to accept a moderately slower way of life had twice resulted in disaster and breakdown: I had driven my broken body too far and caused unnecessary suffering to myself and my family.

Even once I had learned the lesson that I was physically unable to do as much as before, I tormented myself with frustration and envy. Most of our arguments and irritations when we were in London had stemmed from the fact that I wanted to be out there, actively evangelising like the other women, not confined to domestic and family life.

Now, unexpectedly, I found my dilemma solved for me. In the alien environment of the East I was perfectly at ease for the first time since the accident, able to function fully within society. Here in Iran, women were expected to express themselves through hospitality in the home. In the West, where other avenues were open to women, and direct evangelism was possible, I was in conflict: either frustrated by my restrictions or tempted to overtax my strength and make myself ill. Doing God's will may involve different things in different places; here I found it easy to be content with my role.

This realisation brought a great sense of release. I saw how well I fitted into the path God had prepared for me: he had work for me to do, even though I was now disabled. It is hard to accept that 'in all things

God works for the good of those who love him, who have been called according to his purpose' (Rom 8:28)—and it is too easily offered as a facile and meaningless sop to those who are suffering. Yet now I saw that some good had come out of my physical sufferings and spiritual struggles. The difficult obedience which had brought me to Iran had also, unexpectedly, transported me into a culture where my role was as active and fulfilling as I could have hoped.

As our work developed, we began to gain some insights into the Iranian culture and outlook, which proved helpful to us. Iran is a beautiful country of great contrasts: the mountains around Tehran are snow-capped almost all the time, yet they overlook massive salt deserts where little will grow. In between are fertile areas of countryside dotted with orange groves, date trees, and small farms producing vegetables, fruits and nuts. In the towns there are tea gardens, markets and bazaars where all manner of produce can be bought.

This lovely land, positioned as it is at a kind of crossroads in central Asia, has a long history of invasion: its people have been manipulated and downtrodden from the time of Alexander the Great onwards. The depradations of Genghis Khan and the Turkman Empire have been succeeded by the French, the Americans and the Russians vying for possession of the oil fields, Iran's latest rich harvest. This history has developed in the people a fervent nationalistic pride: they will resist any further attempt at invasion of their land or their cultural heritage.

When the last Shah came to power he ruled over a typical middle-eastern economy. All the goods in the shops were home-produced—there was little contact with the West and few imports. Supermarkets, leisure activities, fashion were all unknown, part of an alien Western culture. His father had not in fact been part of the traditional, Islamic hereditary monarchy—he usurped the throne. But he was accepted because initially at least he continued the strict adherence to Islamic law, though he did try to encourage some consideration of economic issues in the country's political life.

The young Shah, however, had been educated in Switzerland, and he wanted to bring his country into the twentieth century, with Western ideas of progress and culture. He had seen the changes which had taken place in neighbouring Turkey, over the last eighty years, and he wanted similar economic success for Iran. He had the potential—the world demand for oil was making Iran a wealthy nation—but he didn't have the time: stocks of oil might last for only thirty years. He had to industrialise Iran fast, or see it return to a desert economy.

On our first visit to Iran we saw it as an isolated, primitive country, ruled by Islam. The women lived a separate life, confined to the home, wearing the chedor (a voluminous cloth covering the face and head). It was almost unheard of for women to hold jobs or public office. When we returned the difference was unbelievable.

In 1966 the Shah had introduced the White Revolution, a twelve-point plan for progress including economic, social and industrial goals, and funded by the increasing oil revenues. He wanted to eradicate illiteracy, exploit the oil and diversify the economic basis of the country to make Iran self-sufficient economically.

The Shah's wife, Queen Farah, helped him in all

this, by setting an example to women. She adopted a fashionable Western style of dress, which was quickly copied by all but the oldest women. She organised groups of young girls to go out to the villages and isolated country communities, to teach reading and writing, and introduced education for girls, as far as was possible in a Muslim context.

The land reforms also had far-reaching effects. Previously, all the most productive land had been in the hands of some ten wealthy families, while the peasants either rented farms or worked the poor land fringing the deserts. The Shah bought the land from the families, divided it up into small parcels and distributed it to the people. It seemed a laudable act of fair distribution. However, many of these fertile areas depended on a complex system of wells and irrigation pipes and ditches which brought the water from the mountains to the plains: the new owners couldn't afford to maintain them, and as a result, much of the land returned to desert once it was in the hands of the peasants.

When we returned to Iran it was to find that many of these changes were already in train. In Tehran the differences were most noticeable: supermarkets had sprung up, and foreign goods were available everywhere—French shoes and Italian dresses, and even eggs from Bulgaria and cheese from Denmark, for food was being imported too. Women went out in the streets alone, wearing Western clothes; they served in shops and took some of the professional jobs; there were even women police officers, who had swapped their chedor for mini skirts.

However, the changes took effect unevenly: the women had more freedom in the cities, but in the countryside the old ways persisted, and the smaller towns were less Westernised than the larger ones. Even within Tehran there were differences: along the main road and in the north of the city, Western standards prevailed; to the south, in the old city and the bazaar area, the traditional lifestyle was in evidence. It was an uncoordinated society, confused and disturbed by its rapid progress.

At first we merely enjoyed the greater degree of freedom for our work and evangelism, but as we moved deeper into the community we became aware of a profound unease. We attended several events at the British Council, and some dinner parties at the homes of businessmen taking Ron's course. Everywhere there was the usual surface admiration of the Shah (every shop, however small or remote, displayed a picture of the Royal Family) but there seemed to be an undercurrent of dissatisfaction, coupled with a fear lest the growing hatred of the Shah should become known.

Some of this was fuelled by the clergy, who thought the Shah dangerous because he had brought so many foreigners into the country. Indeed, much of the new industrialisation had required German and Japanese aid and skills, and the new defence policies involved dependence on the US army and airforce. The Ayatollah Khomeini had by this time fled to Iraq and thence to France, and he sent cassette tapes back to Iran to circulate his teachings. The Shah began to exert pressure to curb the influence of the clergy.

The ordinary people had benefited enormously from the reforms: they had piped water, free education, free medical care and school meals, but this wasn't necessarily important to them. They mistrusted the Western ideology and technology which seemed to them to be invading their country, and they saw people in the cities making money while the countryside was as poor as ever. It seemed to them that the wealth of their country was being given to foreigners, who invaded their land and trampled on their culture. The Shah's ideas had been good, but the pace of change was too fast even for his supporters.

The subsequent revolution of 1978, which expelled the Shah and returned the country of Iran to a fundamentalist Islamic state, happened after we had completed our work for OM and returned to England. Nevertheless, the first stirrings of it were visible to us throughout the latter part of our time there. It was clear that open Christian work would not be possible for much longer.

Meanwhile we were enjoying our time in Iran, with all the freedoms currently available to us. Nathan and Andrew played baseball at school, and we often went to their Little League games. On one occasion we stayed on after their practice, to watch a friend's mother who played women's softball. The boys had never seen a women's game before, but they made no comment until we got home afterwards. Then Nathan suddenly said, 'I didn't know mothers could run!' Well, maybe I wasn't running, but I was doing pretty well. I had learned, in the sympathetic culture of Iran, to keep my activities within my capabilities, though I still made the occasional mistake.

In Isfahan, in the south, there was a Christian hospital run by an Anglican mission, and they employed a girl from our OM team. Whenever Ron was travelling in that direction I would take the opportunity to go with him, and stay for a few days there. I had one or two periods of anxiety—brought on, as usual, by overwork—and the hospital gave me the support I needed. Many of the wives of the doctors working in the hospital suffered similar symptoms, caused by culture shock and the difficulty of adapting in a strange land, and it helped me to meet these English women and to share our problems.

It took a long time to establish our book agency on a properly legal basis in both England and Iran, and meanwhile Ron's work permit expired. This meant that we were back in the old routine of renewing visas periodically, and the authorities were not particularly helpful. The entire family had to leave the country for three days every three months, in order to retain our status as 'visitors'. Once we spent three days in mid winter freezing in a tiny outpost just inside the Turkish border, where we sat round a pot-bellied stove playing monopoly and talking with the villagers. Sometimes we flew from Abadan to Kuwait, where we were entertained by the many Indian believers living there.

Our most memorable trip, however, was made when we decided to accompany a team who were going to work in northern Pakistan. Foolishly, we travelled in June, in the worst of the heat, because I wanted to see a famous local sight: the Afghan desert in bloom.

We drove across northern Iran to Mashad, near the border, and down to Herat in Afghanistan. From Herat we drove south across the desert, spending one restless night in a hotel on the way: we were kept awake by dogs barking outside all night, we were all hot, and the electricity supply failed so that all the fans stopped working. The next day we did indeed see the desert in bloom: a vast expanse of shimmering purple, with acres of wild tulips stretching into the distance. The sight was slightly spoiled for me, however, as I had developed heatstroke, and could only appreciate the beauty between bouts of vomiting and diarrhoea. Ron was furious with me.

'Nancy, we're only half way to Peshawar, and we have to get this team to their destination. When will you learn to be careful with yourself?'

'I don't want to be careful with myself, I want to do things with the rest of you,' I retorted miserably. But I knew we were only going over all the old ground again, and I would have to accept defeat. It simply wasn't fair to inconvenience the team and the family because of my selfish desire to keep up the pace.

The journey to Kabul was cooler, and there I stayed with the children in the home of an American family, while Ron and the team drove on to Peshawar, across the Khyber Pass. I slept and renewed my strength while he was gone, but I knew that my illness had interfered with the schedule, and that I wouldn't be able to cope with the journey back overland. In the end he drove back with the boys, while I flew direct to Tehran.

On the plane, alone, I was very despondent. It seemed that I would never learn; at every turn I was hampering Ron, which was just what I had determined never to do. What was the point of my travelling with him, if I was only going to slow him down?

After a while, though, common sense took over. I'd had to leave Iran, after all, to renew my visa. And in spite of my illness, I had enjoyed the trip, the sights and sounds, and the refreshing enforced rest in Kabul. I leaned back in my seat and thought of all the people I'd met in those few weeks: the shopkeepers who had bargained cheerfully with me in the bazaar; the watchman who slept outside our friends' house, and who had taken such a fancy to Andrew and Nathan that they begged to be allowed to sleep outside with him. Why had I felt so at home there, and why had I managed to get on with the people so well?

Then I realised that like the Iranians they, too, were Muslims, and part of the huge group of Islamic peoples of Central Asia, all with distinct languages and cultures, but all with certain similarities of outlook.

My trip hadn't been a failure: God was preparing within me the seeds of a vision—a vision for outreach much greater than any I had yet contemplated. Who, I wondered, was working among all those tribes and peoples? There must be millions of them, from Albania in the west to Mongolia in the east. Was anyone bringing them the good news of Jesus' love?

Chapter 10

Traditionally, missionary work was a lifetime vocation: you trained, went out to your chosen field and stayed there, except for occasional home leaves, until you retired. Operation Mobilisation, however, introduced an entirely new concept of mission: they trained young people briefly in the basics, and sent them out in teams for short-term work, usually between one and four years. Most learning came through doing—not a new concept, when you consider how Jesus sent out his disciples. This meant that many young people were willing to join in a missionary effort, knowing that their contribution would be for a limited period, though of course many returned again and again.

We had gone out to Iran planning for a four-year stay, and indeed we managed to accomplish all our aims within that period. Our book agency was registered with both the Iranian and British governments, we had been allowed two work permits for full-time staff attached to the agency, and we had developed a series of very promising outlets in the secular book market.

However, by this time Nathan was in the fifth grade—he was ten—and we felt it was time we gave serious thought to the boys' schooling. We explored various possibilities, and eventually gave in to the plan Nathan himself had put forward: that he should be allowed to go to boarding school in England, with Ben Verwer, George's son.

We took him to England, bought his uniform and settled him in the school; apart from a brief attack of cold feet at the last minute he settled happily and wrote enthusiastically of his new friends and various activities. The rest of the family wasn't quite so cheerful. We all missed Nathan, especially Andrew, and Ron and I had never felt entirely at peace with the idea of having the boys spend so much time away from the family. I'd warned Nathan that if he went to boarding school he wouldn't be able to change his mind about it—he would have to stay there for at least a year—so we all settled down to live our lives separately for a while.

We spent that Christmas together in the States, then, while Ron took Nathan back to school in England and went on alone to Iran, I stayed behind with Andrew, as I was having some tests done in hospital. I'd been getting increasingly severe pain in one hip, and my doctor wanted to check whether it could be caused by arthritis: in fact, the good news was that it wasn't arthritis, but the bad news was that there was no treatment available and I would just have to live with the pain.

It was during this period of separation that Ron and I both began to realise that our time in Iran was coming to an end, and that our task there was finished. Even though our fixed-term work was over, we could easily have chosen to stay on, or to move on to Pakistan or elsewhere, but we felt that God was leading us away from both Iran and OM. We had no idea where the Lord would want to use us next, but when we compared notes, we found that we shared the feeling that the time had come to wind up our work.

Andrew and I rejoined Ron in Iran, and there we discussed possible plans for the future, but we agreed to wait until Nathan joined us in the summer before coming to a final decision. So much depended on how he was getting on at school: it would be silly to disturb him if he were completely happy to go on boarding, whatever our feelings about it. That August there was a leaders' conference arranged in Cyprus, and we planned to have a family holiday at the same time. This meant Nathan making his way from Swansea to Cyprus alone, apart from the school and airline supervision we had arranged. I watched him get off the plane with a stewardess: he looked so young, and yet so confident—after all, he'd been flying round the world since he was a baby. He rushed up to me and stuck his arm through mine.

'Well, Mum,' he said, 'I've done my year!'

That sentence told me everything: he loved school, but he hated being away from the family. The decision was made for us—our family needed to be together.

We explained to Nathan that we couldn't leave Iran until we had trained our replacements, but we assured him that when we collected him from school next Christmas, we would be settling in England permanently. He looked rather pensive.

'OK,' he said slowly. 'But you won't write after I go back, and say it'll be Easter, will you?'

We worked hard that autumn to tie everything up so that we could get away before the winter snows hit Turkey. Ron and Andrew went by van with most of our luggage, leaving me behind to settle our housing and sell our furniture. I was so busy that it wasn't until the last moment that I realised what a wrench it was going to be to leave all our friends—and indeed, a whole way of life.

Dr Ahlevi drove me to the airport in his Mercedes: I would have felt rather grand if I hadn't been so sad. Ashraf hugged me with tears in her eyes.

'Goodbye, Nancy,' she said. 'Give our love to Ron and the boys. I'm sorry you are leaving us, but I'm so glad you will all be together again.'

I waved as they drove away, and wondered how long it would be before I saw them again.

I met Ron and Andrew in Germany, and we travelled back to England together. We stopped briefly in Chelsfield to see Auntie Dolf, but soon set off again to hurry to Swansea—we were all anxious to be reunited with Nathan. We borrowed a car from a friend, and collected him and all his baggage from the school. As we drove away I looked round with a sigh of relief. At last we had all our little family together again.

'Well,' said Andrew cheerfully, 'here we all are. What do we do now?' It was a good question.

We rented a house in Swansea while we took stock of our situation. We wanted to be open to God, so that he could show us the next step, and we needed a breathing space, a time of readjustment before we could see our way clearly. Ron and I had long discussions about it: OM had been our family for sixteen years and to leave meant change.

'The thing is,' said Ron, 'we both need more training. Every time we've tried to get it something's happened to prevent us. But I still feel that it's the best way to prepare ourselves to serve God.'

'We seem to have said all this before!' I answered.

'But the training's more important for you. After all, you're going to be the breadwinner: the boys will need me at home for a good few years yet.'

'So which area do we go for?' asked Ron. 'If I went back into engineering I'd need at least two years for retraining—it's seventeen years since I last worked in that field.'

I grinned at him. 'It's no good being impatient. I guess that whatever you choose, you'll take at least two or three years to qualify. And after all, there's no rush. God brought us back to England to see the boys through the main part of their education; we're talking about ten years or so before they're both independent and we'll be free to go back to overseas missionary work.'

Ron sighed. 'I know. But that still brings us back to the same problem: what do we train in to be most effective? Our aim is to go back to work in a Muslim country, agreed?'

I nodded.

'Well,' he went on, 'I reckon that in a few years' time the door will be closed to full-time Christian work in Iran, judging by the feeling we got while we were there. The clergy won't put up with the Shah's reforms for ever, and there'll be a return to the old-style fundamentalist Islam. If that happens, anyone wanting to work in Iran will have to go in with a specific skill to offer.'

'That sounds reasonable,' I said. 'Except that you know you've never really wanted to go back into engineering. I think that as long as we prepare ourselves as best we can, while we're bringing up the children, God will be able to use us when the time comes.'

'Fine,' said Ron. 'But what do we tell our prayer supporters?'

This was a cause for concern. Some good people had been supporting us for sixteen years: it was difficult to have to say to them that we didn't know what we'd be doing next.

For the next six months, from Christmas until the following summer, we considered the question. Ron didn't panic, but I was getting fidgety to say the least! It was hard to wait in faith, not knowing what God wanted us to do. Ron applied for a grant to study as a mature student, and in the end news came: he was awarded a place at London University to study history and Islamics; he would also be able to learn teaching skills.

As if to confirm this leading, we were offered no less than three houses to live in, and we eventually chose a five-bedroomed house in Tunbridge Wells, which is within commuting distance of London. It wasn't ideal—the house was nearly derelict, and almost every window was broken, but we were given lots of furniture to fill it, and Ron found that three months of hard physical work decorating and restoring it was excellent therapy. The boys were soon settled in schools nearby—Nathan at the grammar school and Andrew at the primary school—and we all felt that we'd come to the right place.

Nevertheless, our hearts were still in Central Asia and the Middle East, and we watched television news reports of events there with immense interest. When the Bible Society invited us to spend six weeks in Beirut, teaching and encouraging the Christians there, we jumped at the chance. After eighteen months in England we were glad to get back to the sun, to the relaxed middle-eastern way of life, and to the urgent spiritual demands of life in a Muslim society.

We spent the six weeks living in the mountains, and travelling into the war area. The boys weren't at all disturbed by the signs of a war-torn country that they saw all around them—the ruined houses, the shelling, and the children hardly older than themselves toting rifles. They made friends and played cheerfully among the debris of broken buildings. At night we stood on our balcony and watched the tracer shells arc through the dark sky.

We returned to England at the end of the summer refreshed by our contact with so many valiant and spiritual Christians; Ron and I were content with what we had been able to achieve, and felt peaceful about returning to the job in hand. We were taken by surprise by the boys' reaction.

Andrew started it, struggling resentfully into his school uniform one September morning.

'I hate these stupid clothes,' he said. 'When are we going home, Mum?'

'But, honey, you are home,' I replied. 'Whatever do you mean?'

'He means home to Iran,' explained Nathan. 'England's horrible.'

'I don't understand,' I said helplessly. 'What's wrong? Aren't you happy at school? Haven't you made friends?'

'Oh, we've made friends all right,' said Nathan. 'But they don't understand.'

'No,' chimed in Andrew. 'They think going on holiday to Cornwall's a really big thing—you know, miles and miles away. Anyway, I got on better with the friends I made in Beirut. Can't we go and live there?'

'With a war on?' I said. 'No, I don't think so. I'm

afraid this is where we are and this is where we're staying—for a while at least. You'll just have to try to like it, I'm afraid.

That night I reported this conversation to Ron, and we prayed for our sons. All these arrangements had been made for their sakes, and it seemed hard that they should resent everything so much. After our time of prayer we sat silently together for a while, and then Ron looked up.

'The trouble is,' he said slowly, 'we went back too soon. The boys still think of the Middle East as home, and it was too soon to visit, however much we enjoyed it. The boys need roots, and we've got to establish them here in England—otherwise they'll never feel they belong anywhere.'

I agreed. 'We'll have to refuse the next invitation, however attractive it is,' I said. 'Tell you what—next summer, let's have a holiday in Cornwall!'

Nevertheless, that visit to Beirut reaffirmed for us our love for Muslims. It made us realise that whether or not we were ever able to live in the Middle East again, our role was to pour our love and energy into helping people who could work out there. Even while Ron was busy with his course at the university and I was running the home and caring for the family, we felt this wasn't enough. I was often reminded of my thoughts in the plane as I flew back alone over Central Asia, my concern for all those millions of Muslim people, unreached and untouched by the good news of Jesus Christ.

No one, it seemed, was working among the tribal peoples of Central Asia. There were at least twenty-four different languages and cultures in that vast area: not one had a complete Bible or a viable church. Translators were needed to work on Bibles. Literature and printers, secretaries, and evangelists were needed to produce and distribute them.

An even quicker way of reaching large numbers of Muslims would be by radio—if we could only afford to buy radio time on European broadcasting stations, and find people willing to make the programmes. As usual, the need was for Christians with particular skills—they had to be able to communicate in the right language and understand the culture. Yet we quickly realised that a committed heart was more important than any skill. Much more could be accomplished by men and women who were willing to work for God whatever the price, than by professionals who wanted a safe and precise job description!

We had two main aims: firstly to encourage and organise pioneer evangelism through radio work, translation and actual mission; and secondly to educate the church in the West, to make Christians aware of the existence of these people groups, and teach them how to relate to Muslims at home.

The radio work was the first area to show growth: we spent some time in concentrated prayer, and the result was not just sufficient money to buy radio time, but contact with a possible broadcaster. Peter was a German who spoke fluent Kazakh: his story was fascinating. Moved by Stalin in the Second World War, Peter's family was one of hundreds 'dumped' in Soviet Central Asia and left to starve. The Muslims took care of them when their need was greatest, and after his father's death Peter was adopted and brought up as a Kazakh. When he finally moved back to Germany and rejoined his mother, he knew he owed his life to the Muslims: the way he saw of repaying that debt was to make radio programmes for us, sharing the Word of God with his adopted nation. Once the broadcasting was under way, we managed to send one or two people into the area to monitor the reception: it was difficult to bounce the beams into such a mountainous area, and in addition, the signals were sometimes jammed by official stations.

Our second aim of educating the church about Muslim work also keeps us busy. Most Sundays Ron is speaking at local churches and he often visits university and college Christian Unions, to present them with the needs of Central Asia and to teach them how to befriend Muslims. These activities don't earn any money, but they bring us into contact with many young people, some of whom may be potential workers or future supporters. This year he will be visiting Scotland, Singapore, Korea, Australia, Kenya, Brazil and the United States, teaching and recruiting.

To our original aims has been added a third, which we found to be vital before any other activity could begin: research. Before the needs of a people can be met, someone has to visit them to find out precisely what those needs are. Some of our teams go out not to begin evangelism, but initially to explore the area, to gather information about the language, history, culture and beliefs of the people. We have been amazed to find how varied these can be.

There are something like 180 million Islamic peoples in the area between Albania and Mongolia, spread across eleven time zones. Centuries ago their ancestors came from Turkey, but now, as a result of war, famine and tribal migration, they are scattered across Central Asia; twenty-four individual people groups, each with their own language and culture, and none with more than a handful of believers among them.

Funding our work is an intriguing problem. We have seen how easy it is to touch the emotions of Christians in the West: millions of pounds pour in for relief in times of famine, earthquake or other disaster. Yet there is little interest in evangelism. So often there is an apparent need for political freedom or deliverance from poverty, but in every case the ultimate need is for the proclamation of the gospel, which brings about changes through transformed lives.

We find that many people are curious about Muslims, but few are willing to be involved in working among them. There seems to be a deep fear and hatred of Islam in the Western mind—almost as though the old rivalry of the Crusades is still smouldering. One in six people on earth is a Muslim: will the next generation in the West live in a society ruled by Islamic laws and traditions, as has happened in Pakistan and North Africa? The sad thing is that there has never been a more fruitful time for witnessing to Muslims. For the first time in history hundreds of Iranians, Afghans and North Africans are coming to accept Christ as the Way.

Initially we financed these activities from any excess money given to us: our friends and family were still generously supporting us, and anything we didn't need for our immediate living expenses we passed on to the work, but as the Trust became better known, we realised that we were building up a list of people who were willing to support it specifically, so we separated its funding. We pay no salaries to our staff: all the individuals who join us in the work are supported by their own prayer partners. Some come for short-term work in the field, and then return to their home churches to carry out the second aim, spreading the word about the needs and the work in progress in this area.

We ourselves live as we always have, by faith. We depend on God to supply our income, and he has never failed us. We live from month to month, and try to be balanced in our approach: we don't live in a poverty-stricken style, but neither are we unduly extravagant. God has always been merciful with us, even when we've made foolish decisions! This kind of simple faith living may seem nonsensical to some people, but we know that it's part of the total commitment to which we have been called. There have been times when we've been completely broke, with no money to pay the phone bill or buy food for the week—but as soon as I went ahead and bought what we needed, the money always came in.

A typical example was when our car broke down; we'd made it soldier on for as long as we could, and finally had to admit that it was a write-off. We prayed for a solution to the problem, and waited for God to show us the answer, which certainly didn't lie in our bank balance.

One evening the phone rang: it was a friend who supported us from time to time, and he asked how the work was going. Just before he rang off he asked whether money was coming for a new car.

'Yes, slowly,' I replied, and finished telling him about our plans.

A few minutes later the phone rang again, and Ron answered it. He came back looking bemused. 'That was James again,' he said. 'He says he's got an extra car, and would we be offended if he gave it to us. He says we can sell it if we want and use the money for a new one—but this one's got an MOT and insurance.' Needless to say, we accepted his offer. Such generous giving is an essential part of the ministry in which we're all involved.

A similar instance of timely giving concerned our office accommodation. It hardly seemed a good use of our funds to continue paying at such a rate. We had also bought a small farm just outside the town, hoping to turn it into a training centre to prepare people for living in Central Asia: we planned to teach third-world farming techniques, mechanics, and how to live off the land, as well as Islamics and how to apply Christian living in an Islamic culture. We had several courses there, but we were unable to house our trainees, which was inconvenient. We needed to provide accommodation, but planning permission was refused. We wondered whether we should move north, where property was cheaper, but a brief visit failed to turn up anything suitable.

It was at this point that we were telephoned by a local Christian businessman, who invited Ron to call on him. Over coffee he explained that he owned a commercial farm with cottages and barns attached, and that he wanted to do something to support missionary work. Our need coincided with his, and he ended by offering us free office accommodation in a converted barn, with an adjoining cottage to house a secretary. We were overwhelmed by his generosity, and rejoiced to find how well God cares for his children.

Since the first edition of this book the collapse of Communism has been more apparent. This inevitably has led to many changes for us. During the years of quiet work in the old USSR Ron had begun to sense a growing awareness of the breadth of the growth of the church and the need to mobilise Christians from other lands.

We began to see that the whole Muslim world breaks down into five cultural-linguistic blocs within which there is a church: the Arab, the Indo-Persian, the Malay, the Turkic and the African. Within these there are people that we have termed 'near relatives'. These near relatives are able to understand the languages of their Muslim neighbours, being related in some way to them. They have less culture shock because they come from the same or similar backgrounds and thus are more effective than missionaries coming from the West who find the Muslim mind so strange. There is a high drop-out rate for western missionaries. Churches have less disposable income and people are coming from dysfunctional families. This all adds up to difficulties in maintaining a strong western missionary presence. On the other hand Egyptian, Indian, Philippino, Brazilian, Korean, Mexican and African Christians are now concerned to obey the Lord and take on the task of world evangelism.

The issues however are different. Often these churches do not have the funds for travel and development work. The need to find ways of funding them has become very apparent. In each generation God shows his people the way to move forwards. I believe that the creation of income generation within these new lands is vital. We need the expertise of the western church in doing business to be put at the disposal of the churches in Africa and elsewhere so that they can fund themselves to some degree. We also find that churches which have sponsored and supported missionaries in the past are now looking to use the funds at their disposal more effectively. Instead of a western couple costing some $50,000 to send and maintain, it is more efficient to support ten Africans or Arabs who know the language, live in the culture and can be set free to fulfil the calling that God has placed upon their lives—and all for the same amount.

This new concept was not acceptable to the mission we had founded and so, in 1991, we formed World in Need Associates, a partner of Leadership Training

Resources. This has grown into a major initiator of third world missions and is expanding rapidly. Indian, African, Korean, Arab and many other nationals are playing a role in partnership with some more traditional approaches into the Muslim world.

God has used the suffering and trials that we have gone through to bring us into an enlarged field of service. Now we are involved not just in Central Asia but in all Muslim areas.

Accommodation for World in Need outgrew our five-bedroomed semi-detached house (yet a second time). We searched for six months for appropriate premises within close proximity of our living so we could *finally* separate home and work as we had done with a previous mission we had parented. This time God gave us a lovely, modern-built defunct church building with marvellous facilities.

We had put our house on the market and prayed for *his* choice this time, not ours—He provided a second little unused church—as a free gift in Surbiton. We wanted and needed a UK-based premises but certainly didn't expect provision for one so soon.

Our house sold to a Christian family of six and we fell in love with a near-by town in Sussex where our International co-ordination takes place. Yet another book will fill all our Heavenly Father's goodness, assurance and enjoyment we've found in our haven of rest at home within walking distance of both office and church!

Over the years we have watched events overtake our friends in Central Asia: the Iranian revolution, the invasion of Afghanistan, the Armenian earthquake, the impact of *perestoika* on the Soviet provinces. Meanwhile, our work has developed and grown, but it still largely follows our two original aims.

Nowadays our involvement in radio work is negligible, apart from a little script-writing, but the pioneer evangelism goes on. We have to find the personnel who can slip into the available slots—they may be teachers of English as a foreign language, experts in animal husbandry, vets, doctors, or nurses—and we give them training in Islamics and the local culture.

Throughout the year we run Islamics courses. Ron lectures on many subjects—history, beliefs, and the many cultures of the Islamic peoples—while I help to run the administrative side, sending information to the students before the course.

We also organise language training for our own people—usually in the country of their placement, since theoretical book-learning is too slow a method for evangelists who need to be able to communicate clearly at a personal level. This involves my writing to our contacts in several countries.

Ron teaches at missionary orientation courses for Youth With a Mission, OM, and at All Nations Bible College and others in this country and abroad. He also speaks at various mission conferences. All this takes up a great deal of his time.

The result of all this is that we are busier than ever. I feel that my vision on the aircraft that day is being fulfilled. I prayed for the people of the lands that spread out below me, and now we are beginning to reach out to them and many others.

Ron is constantly travelling and so he retains his contact with Muslim culture, but I haven't been back to the Middle East for ten years, and it's easy to lose that feeling of immediacy. Sometimes I miss the travelling and a sense of being in the middle of things, though I keep closely in touch with letter writing, faxes and e-mail.

In fact, my behind-the-scenes role has become more and more important to me. A few years ago I came full circle and passed my driving test again, and we bought an automatic car so I could ferry our many visitors to and from the airports. Since the boys left home we have a constant stream of guests, and my ministry involves entertaining and hospitality. Just being available in this way means that I am there when people want a listening ear; I can pray over their concerns, aspirations and problems. This concentration on relationships has enriched my share of the work immensely: it's easier to find the right placements for people after they've stayed for a few days in our home.

I don't very often look back along the road that brought us to this point—writing this book has been a curious exercise, uncovering memories which have lain hidden for many years.

It isn't possible for me to forget by disability, because I live with it constantly. It curtails my activities to an irritating extent, especially in the winter months, when I always find the cold and damp particularly debilitating. And one worrying development is that I seem to be losing power in my left hand and side—I don't know whether this can be halted, but I'm taking a course of physiotherapy to strengthen the muscles. I wear a brace at night to straighten my left hand. The pain in my hip joint has never gone away; its cause is unknown, and I sometimes have to take painkillers at night so that I can sleep.

In spite of this I don't reflect much on the accident—it happened a long time ago, and I've got on with life since then, stubbornly refusing to consider myself disabled. I don't think about what life would have been like if it hadn't happened, nor what sort of person I would have been, for I'm sure that whatever the circumstances of our lives, God is able to work through them. There are lessons I've had to learn—of humility, of patience, of perserverence—that I would have had to learn anyway. Most of them I'm still learning, again and again. Surviving the accident didn't transform me into a saint, and I still have to live with my frustration and anger, and sometimes with the results of my own obstinacy. Too often I'm unable to see my own limits—and sometimes I see them but I'm unwilling to stop and inconvenience others.

I believe that God had a plan for my life—the mission work I've done and the work I'm involved in now. When the accident happened, it made it harder for me to fulfil that plan, but it wasn't an excuse to give up or sit back. Like Paul's 'thorn in the flesh' my disability has irritated me, but I've had to accept it. I've had to come through the suffering to do God's will, and I can only give thanks that he can take the circumstances of our lives and use them to his glory. I've seen how wonderfully even my handicaps have fitted into his plan, so that situations I've regarded with dread—like our return to Iran—have been transformed into times of fulfilment and joy. I can trust God to accomplish his purpose, even with the most unlikely person—me!

Over the years, I've learned the necessity of endurance—to keep on keeping on, even in the dark times of emotional stress and physical pain. I have never been abandoned: every time I have recovered, either through prayer or through conventional medicine. Through that I have realised how deeply God cares for each one of us, and that we can trust him, wholeheartedly, with our lives.

I'm not yet completely healed. It may be that I shall never now be whole until I die, when this damaged body will be replaced with a new and glorious body. Yet when I look back at that devastating accident, I marvel at the miracle of healing God has accomplished in me, giving me more than I ever dared to hope. I have not only walked, but travelled all over the world; not only cared for my family, but shared our life with guests and visitors and missionary teams; not only continued in my Christian faith, but shared the good news of Jesus with others in this country and abroad.

Every one of these things I've done by the grace of God: 'I have been crucified with Christ and I no longer live, but Christ lives in me' (Gal 2:20). Even my weakness and the need for physical discipline (remembering that I need proper food and rest in order to keep going) are constant reminders of the need for spiritual discipline (for prayer and Bible reading to sustain the Christian life), emphasising to me my constant dependence on Jesus Christ. 'We have this treasure in jars of clay to show that this all-surpassing power is from God and not from us . . . For we who are alive are always being given over to death for Jesus' sake, so that his life may be revealed in our mortal body' (2 Cor 4:7, 11).

Through hardship, danger and suffering our family has learned to trust God—and that he never lets us down. This assurance is a greater prize than health, or wealth, or any success. It enables us to praise God through all the ups and downs of everyday life, and makes me realise what a blessing it can be to suffer— when that suffering draws us closer to God.

I know that ours is a privileged position: we have personally encountered the multitudes who have no vision of Christ. It is the burden of concern we bear for these people which inspires us to work and to call others to share our efforts. We know from experience that the work of Christian mission is not romantic, but is rewarding—and the greatest reward of all is to know that you are working within the will of God. Whatever you are doint with the life God has given you, consider giving it back to him, not half-heartedly, but handicaps and all. Fresh, cool, living water is just as satisfying from a marred clay pot as from a perfect one.

Addresses

If you would like to make contact with Nancy George or World In Need Associates, please write, phone or fax to the following address:

UK

World in Need Associates
(A division of Leadership Training Associates)
PO Box 109
Crowborough
East Sussex
TN6 2ZN

Tel: 01892-669834
Fax: 01892-669894
e-mail: win@pavilion.co.uk

USA

World in Need Associates
PO Box 1525
Oak Park
ILLINOIS 60304

Tel: 708-524-9474
Fax: 708-524-9119
e-mail: 102705.2651@compuserve.com